Developing Non-Hierarchical Leadership on Campus

Recent Titles in
The Greenwood Educators' Reference Collection

Developing Non-Hierarchical Leadership on Campus

Case Studies and Best Practices in Higher Education

Edited by
Charles L. Outcalt, Shannon K. Faris,
and Kathleen N. McMahon

Foreword by Alexander W. Astin

The Greenwood Educators' Reference Collection

GREENWOOD PRESS
Westport, Connecticut • London

Library of Congress Cataloging-in-Publication Data

Developing non-hierarchical leadership on campus : case studies and best practices in
  higher education / edited by Charles L. Outcalt, Shannon K. Faris, and Kathleen N.
  McMahon ; foreword by Alexander W. Astin.
     p. cm.—(The Greenwood educators' reference collection, ISSN 1056–2192)
   Includes bibliographical references and index.
   ISBN 0–313–31178–1 (alk. paper)
    1. Educational leadership—United States—Case studies. 2. Leadership—Study and
  teaching (Higher)—United States—Case studies. 3. Civic leaders—Training of—United
  States—Case studies. I. Outcalt, Charles L., 1964– II. Faris, Shannon K., 1973– III.
  McMahon, Kathleen N., 1964– IV. Series.
  LB2806.D437   2001
  378'.01—dc21   00–027630

British Library Cataloguing in Publication Data is available.

Library of Congress Catalog Card Number: 00–027630
ISBN: 0–313–31178–1
ISSN: 1056–2192

First published in 2001

Greenwood Press, 88 Post Road West, Westport, CT 06881
An imprint of Greenwood Publishing Group, Inc.
www.greenwood.com

Printed in the United States of America

The paper used in this book complies with the
Permanent Paper Standard issued by the National
Information Standards Organization (Z39.48–1984).

10 9 8 7 6 5 4 3 2 1

Contents

Foreword

Alexander W. Astin

The problems that plague modern American society—growing economic inequities, the disappearance of community, excessive materialism, decaying inner cities, racial tensions, a deteriorating infrastructure, environmental degradation, a troubled public school system, declining civic engagement, and the increasing ineffectiveness of government, to name a few—are in many respects problems of leadership. By "leadership" I mean not only what elected and appointed public officials do, but also the critically important civic work performed by those individual citizens who are actively engaged in making a positive difference in society. Clearly, one of the major problems with contemporary civic life in America is that too few of our citizens are actively engaged in efforts to effect positive social change.

While many scholars in the academy are actively engaged in analyzing our various societal ills, they seldom acknowledge higher education's possible contribution to these problems or the role that it might play in alleviating them. It is difficult to overstate the importance of the role that higher education plays in shaping the quality of leadership in modern American society. Our colleges and universities not only educate each new generation of leaders in government, business, science, law, medicine, the clergy, and other advanced professions, but are also responsible for setting the curriculum standards and training the personnel who will educate the entire citizenry at the pre-collegiate level. Like it or not, we are a central player—perhaps the central player—in the development of "future leaders."

Our 3,500 colleges and universities provide rich opportunities for recruiting and developing leaders through the curriculum and co-curriculum. Co-curricular experiences not only support and augment the students' formal classroom and curricular experience, but can also create powerful learning opportunities for leadership development through collaborative group projects that serve the institution or the community. These projects can be implemented through service learning, residential living, community work, and student organizations.

Although the catalogs and mission statements of many colleges and universities frequently mention educational goals such as "preparing leaders for the future" and "developing social and civic responsibility," there is little evidence of any interest in these goals either in our undergraduate general education curricula or in our pedagogy. The principal exceptions to this general neglect of leadership by our higher education institutions are, of course, the excellent student leadership development programs that are operated by the student affairs staffs in many hundreds of our colleges and universities. Some of the most innovative of these programs have been developed by the contributors to this volume.

American higher education has traditionally defined a "student leader" either as someone who occupies a formal student office (e.g., student body vice-president or editor of the student paper) or as someone who has achieved visibility on the campus by virtue of athletic or some other form of achievement. This rather narrow approach not only relegates most students to the role of "non-leader," but also creates an implicit "leader-follower" hierarchy which, in the minds of most students, greatly limits their notions of who can or should "lead." The great power of the non-hierarchical approach to student leadership that characterizes this book is that it expands the number of potential "student leaders" to include virtually all students, while simultaneously transforming the *process* by means of which leadership is exercised on the campus.

While many treatises on "leadership" are written by scholars who tend to focus primarily on conceptual and theoretical issues, a distinguishing feature of this book is that it is written primarily by practitioners who are sharing real-life experience that they have acquired while working in the trenches of student leadership development. The variety of institutional settings where these programs are in operation is remarkable: major public research universities, urban universities, private universities, public four-year colleges, an Ivy League college, a community college, and Roman Catholic colleges and universities.

Another major strength of this book is the variety of approaches taken to discussing issues of non-hierarchical student leadership development, which include case studies, program descriptions, outcome evaluations, and several theoretical/conceptual essays covering a diversity of topics ranging from feminist perspectives on the concepts of "citizenship" and "community" to new models for designing and operating student leadership development programs.

More than a dozen of the chapters discuss various applications of the Social Change Model of Leadership Development (Higher Education Research Institute [HERI], 1996), a non-hierarchical, value-based approach to leadership development which has been adopted recently by many student affairs practitioners who are engaged in student leadership development. The versatility and flexibility of this model is apparent in the many different contexts in which it has been applied in the various chapters; formal courses on leadership, leadership retreats, community service, orientation programming, strategic planning, staff training, assessment, and leadership training programs with a variety of foci (diversity/multicultural, sexual orientation, gender, international/global, etc.).

Given our American penchant for ranking and rating just about everything from television shows and athletic teams to political candidates and even colleges and universities, the notion of a non-hierarchical approach to leadership is going to be a "hard sell." Even our higher education institutions reinforce the notion of hierarchy, what with their hierarchical administrative structures, faculty "ranks," hierarchical forms of student government organization, and strong emphasis on competition. Nevertheless, a careful examination of the very interesting chapters comprising this book should convince even the most skeptical reader that a non-hierarchical approach not only is feasible, but also offers us opportunities to substantially expand and strengthen our collegiate programs for student leadership development.

REFERENCE

Higher Education Research Institute. (1996). *A Social Change Model of Leadership Development* (3rd ed.). Los Angeles: Author.

Introduction

Several years ago, we were charged with the privilege and responsibility of creating the Bruin Leaders Project, UCLA's non-hierarchical leadership development program based on the Social Change Model (SCM) of Leadership Development. While we found many excellent resources to help us move from our theoretical knowledge of and faith in the tenets of non-hierarchical leadership, we could not find one central source to meet our needs. How useful it would be, we imagined, if we could have in our hands a single volume filled with theoretical explorations of non-hierarchical leadership, reflections from key thinkers in this field, case studies of successful campus programs, and insights into assessing the program we were devising. Whether you are a student exploring your own leadership development, a student affairs practitioner contemplating a new program or fine-tuning one that is already in existence, a faculty member teaching leadership, or simply an individual interested in the possibility of reconsidering and re-envisioning the way you lead, we hope this volume meets your needs.

Before we outline the contents of this volume, we would like to call attention to one particular feature. We have realized that no one speaks more articulately or eloquently about student leadership development than students themselves. Accordingly, we have included student voices as often as possible throughout this volume. Many authors have used quotations in their chapters to what we feel is very strong effect. In addition to these chapter-specific voices, you will find brief excerpts taken from the meditations of UCLA students on non-hierarchical leadership in general and their experience in the Bruin Leaders Project in particular. We hope these passages speak as strongly to you as they do to us on the pressing need to instill in students (and in ourselves) a notion of leadership that promotes teamwork, honors diversity, and brings out the best talents of all members of the group.

The book is presented in four sections. Section I, on theory, sets a framework for thinking about non-hierarchical leadership. Section II, on the practice of non-hierarchical leadership, offers eleven case studies. Section III explores various issues of student identity, as it relates to leadership development. Lastly and importantly, we conclude with a section on assessment.

Section I: Thinking about Non-Hierarchical Leadership Development. While the focus of this volume is on practice, we thought it essential not only to include a section on theory, but to include as broad a perspective on thinking about non-hierarchical leadership as possible. A single chapter on the historical perspectives that have brought leadership theory to its current state might have given useful background but would not have provided a voice for the evolution of our understanding of what it means to "lead." To ensure a diversity of perspectives on this evolution and its results, we have included complementary but contrasting chapters on leadership theory. Accordingly, Section I of this book opens with an interview with Helen S. Astin, co-author of the groundbreaking *Women of Influence, Women of Vision*, in which she and her co-author examined three generations of participants in the women's movement, and one of the founding members of the Working Ensemble that developed the SCM. In this interview, Dr. Astin shares her evolving insights on leadership, especially as practiced by and developed in students. Faris and Outcalt's chapter offers a historical perspective on leadership theory in general, beginning with the very origin of the term. Leadership theorists Yammarino and Dansereau offer a taxonomy for organizing and understanding contemporary leadership theory in Chapter 3. Moving from the broad field of leadership to specific approaches and models, Bonous-Hammarth describes the SCM in some detail in Chapter 4. Cherrey and Allen provide a provocative view of the challenges of leadership and life in a postmodern era in Chapter 5. The section ends with Varlotta's richly historicized and tightly argued critique of current non-hierarchical leadership theory and proposes yet another means of conceptualizing leadership.

Section II: Putting Theory into Action: Successful Campus Programs. While there are as many ways of practicing non-hierarchical leadership development successfully as there are campuses, we have included several case studies of particularly interesting programs in the second section of this book. Separately, each of these provides a useful example of one way of introducing the principles of non-hierarchical leadership into student development programs; together, these case studies illustrate the breadth of programming possible when we dare to rethink our understanding of leadership. Green, Alexander, and Boryczka offer insights on teaching leadership theory and practice gleaned from their experience with a graduate degree program in leadership development. Roberts provides an account of large-scale institutional transformation made possible at Miami University of Ohio through the use of the SCM. Robertson and Lubic's chapter describes a highly successful collaborative effort between academic and student affairs organizations to bring the SCM to their campus, as does Martin's story of the implementation of the SCM at her institution. Cherrey, Garbuio, and Isgar provide another perspective on institution-wide leadership development in their description of several programs that span the all too common gap between academic and co-curricular activities. Continuing to expand on the role of the classroom in developing leadership, Huber provides an account of a leadership development course employing a hybrid non-hierarchical leadership development model. A programmatic description from a private Catholic institution is offered by Bischetti. Following the programmatic vein, Langdon and Mathias provide useful tips for teaching the SCM and other forms of non-hierarchical leadership. Moving to the realm of community colleges, staff and faculty from Paradise Valley Community College in Phoenix describe their innovative use of the SCM within a multifaceted orientation program, while Klumpyan and Langdon write honestly of their experience in using the SCM in advising students, sharing a nearly perfect and a more "realistic" account of two experiences they have had in their role as advisors. In more specialized and highly useful examples of successful non-hierarchical leadership programming, Liscinsky, Chambers, and Foley recount the implementation of the SCM in a residential life example, while Zavala-Corzo concludes this section by describing the means by which she and her colleagues introduced the principles of non-hierarchical leadership into advising for international students.

Section III: The Complex Intersections of Leadership and Identity. In our work with UCLA's wonderfully diverse student body, we have realized that leadership must include the entire student in all of his or her complexity, and so it was vital for us to include chapters on the complex intersection of leadership and identity. In the third section of this volume, you will find a thought provoking chapter by Adams and Aqui on the importance of recognizing and honoring cultural differences when developing leadership and another from Millette and Fisher describing a challenging and ultimately transformative leadership and awareness program. Sanlo's chapter on leadership and identity, especially for lesbian, gay, bisexual, and transgender students, rounds out this section.

Section IV: How We Define and Measure Success: Assessing Leadership Development. Many of the case studies included in this volume highlight assessment and evaluation as integral program components. As funding sources for co-curricular and curricular programs tighten and the demand for accountability in the form of outcomes information increases, evaluation and assessment have become imperative. This is particularly true of programs that utilize new and nontraditional models such as non-hierarchical leadership. The final section of this volume provides two chapters that explore the assessment and evaluation of non-hierarchical leadership. In Chapter 22 Cress provides a framework for considering program assessment that is congruent with the distinctive characteristics of non-hierarchical leadership. Tyree follows this with a practical discussion on the implementation of programmatic evaluation framed by a description of her development of the only instrument created to date expressly to assess the Social Change Model.

We would like to acknowledge the steadfast and generous support of Robert J. Naples, UCLA's Assistant Vice Chancellor of Student and Campus Life and Dean of Students, for believing in the Bruin Leaders Project, from the time it was merely a hope, and for supporting us in all the ways it counted. His faith and advocacy for innovative student programming made the vision become a reality.

This volume is dedicated to the students of the Bruin Leaders Project, especially to those members of the Student Facilitation Team, whose voices we have included throughout the volume, who have touched our thoughts and our lives with their creativity, talent and energy. Their open minds and hearts and willingness to re-envision leadership have given us hope about the next generation of leaders.

Section I

Thinking about Non-Hierarchical Leadership Development

REFLECTIONS FROM UCLA STUDENT JOE MANKO

Reimagining leadership, from the foundation up, starts with the idea that everyone has the potential for being a leader. Each individual possesses the ability to lead in his or her own unique way, and consequently, contributions from everyone, whether in an organization, community, or society are essential to an efficiently working whole. Nonhierarchical leadership stems from the realization that every individual contribution is important for societal advancement. It is a return to the statement "I can make a difference, what I say is important, and in promoting social change I am a leader."

The notion that everyone possesses the ability to lead in his or her own unique way forms the foundation for thought on nonhierarchical leadership. A second realization in the reimagining of leadership is that leadership is neither power nor position reserved for an elite few, but rather a process that can be experienced by all individuals. This second aspect of nonhierarchical leadership challenges the traditional belief in positional models by developing an inclusive environment in which everyone is welcome to express his or her thoughts and insights.

Chapter 1

An Interview with Helen S. Astin

Kathleen N. McMahon

Ms. McMahon. You have been writing about leadership for the past couple of decades. Given this experience, how do you define leadership?

Dr. Astin. Leadership is a collective effort of persons who care about an issue, a situation, who feel passionate about it, and who work together toward change, change that benefits everyone, change for the common good.

Ms. McMahon. You have co-authored a book on women leaders, *Women of Influence, Women of Vision* (1991). How do you believe that leaders learn to lead?

Dr. Astin. First of all, the question is a bit jarring to me because I don't think leaders lead. I have a different conception of leadership that is much more collaborative. As I said earlier, leadership is when someone cares about something, feels that something needs to change, improve, and engages other like-minded people to work on it together. I am thinking in terms of leadership and social change; leadership, that improves the quality of life for people, or changes an institution to make it a better place. So change is very central to leadership. What I see as the role of the individual, is to involve others and to engage with them in a process of social change. Well, how does this person learn to do that? which is the question you asked, I think. You might have learned how to lead collaboratively by having done it before and having learned from your own experience what has worked and what hasn't worked, based on your experience. You also learn from role models by seeing others engage in the process of leadership.

I have also thought a lot about what leadership development should entail. I think academic knowledge is important—in a sense, understanding group dynamics and having a better understanding of how organizations work are essential. That is, having knowledge and an intellectual understanding. But most importantly, leadership is about being aware of your values and engaging in the process and learning through the process—learning how to collaborate, how to be a good listener, how to be empathic. There are some things that you learn by doing and some things you learn by reading and reflecting. So I see both components. And of course, becoming aware of some of the gifts you have, personally. Rather than saying you are genetically endowed with leadership talent, just being aware of who you are and what your talents are because we all have gifts.

Ms. McMahon. How do you see your work in *Women of Influence, Women of Vision* pertaining to: (1) higher education as an institution, and (2) students and student development?

Dr. Astin. Working on the book *Women of Influence, Women of Vision* is where I learned that leadership is a collective effort. I learned that people who engage in leadership are self-aware, feel committed, and collaborate with others in accomplishing changes in institutions and in society at large, regarding issues of equity, inclusion and justice. That study and what we learned from it informed our work in developing the Social Change Model of Leadership Development. As you know the model identifies seven values that are central to leadership. Most of these values were observed with the women leaders in our study of *Women of Influence, Women of Vision*. The seven values in the social change leadership model are self-awareness, congruence/authenticity, commitment, being able to work collaboratively, shaping a common purpose, dealing with conflict and controversy with civility, and exercising citizenship (being a member of a group, the society, with all the privileges and responsibilities it entails).

I see these values as being essential to how we should organize and do our work within higher education institutions; these elements/principles are essential in both, higher education leadership and in leadership development for students.

Ms. McMahon. You have anticipated my next question perfectly. Can you discuss what you see as the essential components of a leadership program?

Dr. Astin. I believe very strongly in making people aware of who they are, what they observe, and what they experience. Being very aware, very mindful of what is happening. A reflection on what we are learning is essential. Definitely, a leadership program should have a reflective component, keeping a reflective journal. To me so much of it is making people aware—processing what they experience. Helping people become particularly aware of what works and what does not work.

Ms. McMahon. What about having role models? What part can they play?

Dr. Astin. Again, it goes back to making people self-aware. We all admire people, but I don't know how aware we are about what it is that we admire.

Ms. McMahon. That is interesting because when I consider the significance of role models, I think first about significant people that I can admire. Maybe we pattern ourselves after these people, but not entirely consciously.

Dr. Astin. I feel very strongly that you need to develop consciousness of self, an awareness of who you are, what you value, and what you believe in. You can't say, I'll be like this person because this person looks interesting and suc-cessful. It has to come from you, from within you.

Ms. McMahon. Let us turn now to another important concept in leadership, the notion of empowerment. What kinds of things help people feel empowered? What would you do to help them bring that about?

Dr. Astin. First of all, once students understand what leadership is, they need to see how they can engage other people collaboratively, and how they can be good listeners. And they need to own who they are and what their strengths are. That is very empowering. Empowerment is exactly what happens in a collab-orative group, in terms of how everybody's opinion is valued and everybody is allowed to express themselves and be heard. In our book, *Women of Influence, Women of Vision*, we quote from Carl Rogers about the process of empowerment (Astin & Leland, 1991, p. 9). According to Rogers some of the things we can do to empower others include giving autonomy to persons and groups, delegat-ing with full responsibility, freeing people to "do their thing," expressing one's own ideas and feelings as one aspect of the group data, facilitating learning, stimulating independence in thought and action, accepting the "unacceptable" innovative creations that emerge, offering and receiving feedback, encouraging and relying on self-evaluation, and finding rewards in the development and achievements of others.

Ms. McMahon. Could you comment about your recent Kellogg Foundation-sponsored project on leadership?

Dr. Astin. I serve on a Kellogg Foundation sponsored Task Force on Lead-ership. A number of us on the Task Force had served as an advisory review panel for Kellogg before, assisting the Foundation in their efforts to encourage institutions and community agencies to develop leadership programs for college age youth. Our current effort, to some extent, is a continuation of that work, and it involves the development of a monograph, *Leadership Reconsidered*, addressing the practice of transformative leadership for all members of the ac-ademic community: administrators, faculty and students. By transformative lead-ership we have adopted language used by The Kellogg Foundation: "leadership that helps us create a world in which each person has a sense of worth; accepts responsibility for self, family, community and societal well-being; and has the capacity to be productive, and to help create nurturing families, responsible institutions, and healthy communities."

Ms. McMahon. How do current non-hierarchical leadership models fit with other current initiatives such as service learning?

Dr. Astin. My sense of non-hierarchical models is that such programs are centered on valuing everyone; every person has something to contribute that is essential to leadership. Non-hierarchical models are based on collaboration. Self-awareness is essential to non-hierarchical leadership. To be self-aware you need to be reflective. And to collaborate you need to be caring, to be able to trust, to be a good listener and to be empathic. In service learning, it is crucial that you reflect. It is only then that understanding and learning take place as a result of your service. And your service improves because you know more and you have a better understanding of the social context and of the people you serve. Reflection makes you more aware. I believe that learning happens when the person who serves collaborates with those who are being served, as equal partners, with trust, respect and empathy.

Ms. McMahon. As we contemplate differences in leadership styles that are somehow associated with personal characteristics, such as gender, how can we avoid making an almost essentialist assumption that there is an inevitable and predictable link between these characteristics and leadership styles? In other words, how can we talk about a "women's" way of leading, for example, without assuming that (1) all women lead in the same way, and (2) that this way is related to their social position as women? Where does a construct such as "women's leadership" leave room for cultural variation within women as a group, and for the use of "women's leadership" style by men?

Dr. Astin. This question is a very complicated one. It could be an essay in itself. "Is there a women's way of leading?" Are women inherently different? More collaborative? Able to share power and exercise leadership in non-hierarchical ways?

Most studies that have looked at women's leadership have identified a non-hierarchical, collaborative style of leadership. My feeling is that this is indeed the case, that women find it easier to collaborate and to share power. Also, my impression is (and it is also supported by research) that women are better listeners and exercise more caring in their relationships. Leading relationally is easier for women. And I believe that this is a consequence of socialization and of differences in the experiences of women as compared to men—be it at home or at work, rather than genetically or biologically determined differences. Women are expected to be the nurturers, to take care of children, elderly parents, people at work, those who work for them, peers, or even their supervisors. They have had a long training in how to listen and how to care. While we may say that more women than men find it easier to collaborate and exercise non-hierarchical leadership, it is not to say that all women are like that or that they behave in that way. There is ample evidence that there are plenty of differences within women, and I am sure that many of us have seen and dealt with women who have been autocratic and unwilling to share their power.

Ms. McMahon. How, exactly, can we practice non-hierarchical leadership styles within predominantly hierarchical environments, such as colleges and universities? Even if we can create non-hierarchical "spaces" within these institutions, how do we navigate at the border between those new spaces and the traditional environment?

Dr. Astin. This is one of the most difficult issues facing those who are in the business of working with students in leadership development programs. How are students to understand and negotiate the institutional hierarchy while they have come to recognize the importance of behaving in non-hierarchical ways and to engage in collaboration? How? They have to model the way. They have to demonstrate non-hierarchical leadership by their words and deeds. But also they have to be knowledgeable of organizations, know and understand organizational theory and organizational practices; they need to understand the dynamics of power in organizations and why people in authority act in authoritarian, non-hierarchical fashion. If students can come to understand that within hierarchical structures they can assume responsibility and exercise leadership without dominance, then they can begin to integrate the principles of non-hierarchical leadership with an effective transformation of organizational practice. We as instructors and advisors must model this realization ourselves. Knowledge and understanding on one hand and being true to one's principles of non-hierarchical, collaborative leadership on the other hand can help students negotiate the system and at the same time teach others by modeling this different, relational, collaborative kind of leadership.

Ms. McMahon. Where do you believe leadership, in general, is going? For example, if you were asked to write an essay for the Leader of the Future, what would it be about and why?

Dr. Astin. As I look at the social, political and economic issues that affect our lives now and as we begin the new millennium, I think of three very critical forces that are shaping our society and forcing us to examine the way we do our work and relate to each other. One is globalization and diversity. We are becoming more diverse, seeing and experiencing different cultures, interacting with people from different backgrounds, different experiences, different needs. The second issue is interdependence—we are all connected, we all share the global environmental and economic concerns. These global issues should be an important part of the leadership agenda. Third is the growth of technology—it provides us with easy access to knowledge and to each other; it can be/is a blessing but also raises a number of questions about inequities, distancing us from one another and perhaps damaging interpersonal relationships, isolating us and making us vulnerable to systems that can crash at anytime. Given these forces, what then should be the qualities, skills, attributes of future leaders? My list, not an exhaustive one, includes global knowledge and understanding, the ability to transcend personal interests for the benefit of others, being and becoming of the community, exercising empathy, being self-aware, congruent, and authentic, and working on how to empower others. I believe that the kind of leadership that is required to meet the challenges facing us is a leadership that is servant, caring and ethical; a collaborative and multidirectional rather than top-down, hierarchical leadership; a leadership that is knowledgeable about other cultures and global concerns; one that posses a cross-cultural, cross-national understanding.

Ms. McMahon. If you could give the keynote address to a nationwide televised graduate ceremony to all colleges and universities, what would you tell them about the importance of leadership and non-hierarchical leadership, in particular?

Dr. Astin. Oh, this question also requires a whole essay in itself, not a paragraph. But let me try. What would I say at a graduation ceremony about leadership? Remember, each one of you is a leader. You are asked to be a leader and do leadership work in every place you find yourself in. But to be a leader that makes a difference you need to trust yourself and trust those you work with. You need to listen to them, learn from them, bring the best out in them. You cannot do this important work alone. But most of all, remember that we are called to do work that can make this world, this place, a better place, for all of us. And in that, we need each other, we need all the talent, energy and good will. In the words of Sebastiáo Salgado,

> All of life is a collaboration. The destiny of men and women is to create a new world, to reveal a new life, to remember that there exists a frontier for everything except dreams. In history, there are no solitary dreamers, one dreamer breathes life into the next.

REFERENCE

Astin, H. S., & Leland, C. (1991). *Women of influence, women of vision: A cross-generational study of leaders and social change*. San Francisco: Jossey-Bass.

Chapter 2

The Emergence of Inclusive, Process-Oriented Leadership

Shannon K. Faris and Charles L. Outcalt

James MacGregor Burns captured the current status of leadership theory in writing: "Leadership is one of the most observed and least understood phenomena on earth" (1978, p. 2). While space will not permit us to examine the development of leadership theory in its entirety, a brief, multidisciplinary review of some major developments would provide a useful context for the explorations of non-hierarchical leadership found throughout this volume. In this review, we will be concerned particularly with the emergence of what is often known as the "post-industrial" leadership paradigm, a term we will refrain from defining precisely at present, for reasons which will become apparent shortly. Our discussion will be arranged more or less chronologically, from the most traditional understandings of leadership to the most recent and compelling.

TRADITIONAL "INDUSTRIAL" MODELS

The Military Theory

In the Military theory, the leader assumes control of the group and takes responsibility for the actions of each of its members. The leader's control is exercised hierarchically—in other words, each group member is responsible for following the member above him or her in the group's structure, with ultimate control residing with the overall leader. In this theory, the leader is the focus of the group and its practices (Bass, 1981) and is in a privileged position relative to other group members. Military leaders are (or seek to be) *in control*. The Military theory can be traced as far back as *The Republic*, in which Plato described this as one of three modes of leadership (along with the models of philosopher/statesman [*sic*] and the businessman [*sic*] meeting the material needs of the populace) (Bass, 1981, p. 17). Elements of this theory can be found in the *Iliad* as well, in which Homer applauds Achilles's valor and action (Bass, 1981). Rogers (1996) summarizes this theory succinctly. For her, the military model features a leader who "operates from a top-down philosophy and is decisive, efficient, tough-minded, unemotional and in-control" (Rogers, 1996, p. 243).

As is evident from the above description, the Military theory of leadership features one person at the center of a group, or to use an even more apt metaphor, at the top of a pyramid comprised of followers. Historically, this theory has nearly always depended on a male, usually white, leader, from Homer to Machiavelli to Napoleon.

The Military theory shares some elements with the Great Man [*sic*] theory, which can be understood as forming a link between it and the Trait theory, described below. The Great Man theory states that some individuals have a greater natural endowment of those characteristics that lead to leadership. However, as Bass (1981) notes, the Great Man theory contains a thread of belief in Darwinism and the notion that leadership ability is passed from generation to generation genetically. This belief in the inherited nature of leadership creates an affinity between the Great Man theory and arguments for monarchical rule—if leadership is inherited, it would be only natural that kings would be born of kings. For this reason, the Great Man theory, with its assumption that only a chosen few are able to lead, is a natural ally to elitism. Both the Military and Great Man theories, with their emphasis on dominance and control, offer little to those interested in creating or contributing to a diverse, pluralistic society.

The Trait Model

According to the Trait theory, which was predominant early in the twentieth century, leaders are those individuals who have "a natural ability to lead" (Komives, Lucas, & McMahon, 1998, p. 36). These "leaders" are thought to have personal characteristics that make them better leaders. The exact nature of these traits is open to interpretation and varies a great deal from theorist to theorist and study to study. Bass provides an overview of those who have attempted to delineate these traits, from Bernard (1926) to Bird (1940), as well as an extensive analysis of those traits that were considered important by each theorist. Despite the lack of agreement on leadership traits, some characteristics recur again and again: intelligence, height, appearance, athleticism, and eloquence (among others; for details, see Bass, 1981, pp. 48–72). Despite their differences, the Military, Great Man and Trait theories share a common belief that leadership is something with which individuals are born; in this view, leadership is a birthright, rather than a skill to be developed.

As Komives et al. note, the Trait theory fails to withstand critical scrutiny for several reasons: the supposedly relevant traits have never been settled conclusively; once identified they are difficult to measure; and there is no proof that they are related to leadership. Perhaps most damaging to the Trait theory, there is no provision for consideration of the *situation* in which the leader attempts to lead. This deficiency was noted by Stogdill, who called attention to the importance of the situation in which a leader was attempting to lead.

In summary, a chief difference between the Military and Trait theories of leadership (as well as the Great Man theory that can be understood as linking them) and the new theories to come is that the earlier models focused exclusively on the leader and not enough on the people and contexts with which she/he attempted to lead. In Bass's words: "Earlier theorists . . . failed to consider the interaction between individual and situational variables" (1981, p. 6). Komives et al. describe this shift succinctly: "[In the new paradigm] [w]hat a leader does became more interesting than what a leader is" (p. 38).

Behavioral and Style Theories

During the 1950s and 1960s, Behavioral or Style theories emerged from the study of management. These approaches compare "effective" and "ineffective" leadership practices as a means of discerning the one right way to practice leadership (Northouse, 1997). The behavioral and style theories differ from earlier approaches in their emphasis on situations rather than personality traits. Context and the relationship of followers are also considered in these theories. However, the Style and Behavioral approaches have been criticized as ignoring situational variables and the importance of group process (Komives et al., 1998).

Situational and Contingency theories began to develop in the 1950s and remained popular through the 1980s. These theories take into account the environment and situation in which leadership occurs. They recognize that leadership is and must be practiced across diverse contexts (Bass, 1981).

Influence theories arose in the 1920s and maintained influence through the 1970s. With his research on charismatic leadership, Max Weber (1947) is the theorist most closely associated with the development of influence theories. Interest in this type of leadership grew from religious, social, and political movements in which leaders emerged during crises. Robert House formalized the theory of charismatic leadership in 1977 with the development of a testable set of variables meant to predict charismatic personalities (Northouse, 1997). This approach suggests that charismatic leaders possess several unique behavioral approaches that garner follower support. They are said to be strong role models, competent, have the ability to articulate ideological objectives with moral undertones, communicate high expectations for followers, and have the ability to "arouse task-relevant motives in followers that include power, and esteem" (Northouse, 1997, p. 132). While this approach has remained popular with theorists, it has been criticized as being elitist and exclusive (Bass, 1981; Northouse, 1997). The Military, Great Man, Trait, Behavioral, Situational/Contingency, and Influence theories have shaped the dominant view of effective leadership during most of the twentieth century (Rogers, 1996). Rost (1991) has labeled these leadership approaches as falling under the industrial paradigm. Each of these approaches emphasizes the role of leaders in leadership, but they neglect, to varying degrees, the role of the follower. The term *industrial* stems from organizational theories that arose as a result of the industrial revolution in which organizations were viewed as rational-bureaucratic. This view places importance on hierarchical authority and position, division of labor, standardized task operations, rules, and control (Kuh, 1996).

THE EMERGING POST-INDUSTRIAL LEADERSHIP PARADIGM

For Rogers, the new leadership paradigm first received widespread recognition in 1978, when James McGregor Burns pointed to the difference between conventional and transformational leadership modes (Rogers, 1996, p. 243). Much of the emerging leadership paradigm is encompassed by this prescient statement although, as will be outlined, the emerging paradigm was to develop considerably after Burns's foreshadowing. According to Hesselbein, Goldsmith, and Beckhard (1996), new leadership models must be understood in the context of a flattened hierarchy. This insight sets the stage for the new leadership paradigms discussed below—each depends on a rejection of the idea that top-down, pyramidal structures best exemplify leadership. In the following discussion, we will relate Rost's notion of the importance of the relationship between leaders and their communities and will then describe a series of leadership models that move progressively further from the Military, Great Man, and Trait paradigms described above.

ROST'S INTERCONNECTEDNESS/POST-INDUSTRIAL PARADIGM

In his *Leadership for the Twenty-First Century*, Rost (1991) presents a view of leadership that moves beyond the industrial paradigm. He criticizes the industrial theories as inadequate in explaining leadership because, for him, the relationship between leaders and the community is paramount to leadership. In his words, "Leadership is an influence relationship among leaders and their collaborators who intend real changes that reflect their mutual purposes" (1993, p. 99). In other words, leadership is the outcome of the necessary and reciprocal relationship between leaders and collaborators. In the next section of this chapter, we will explore theories that interrogate and privilege the leader/community relationship further, often making it central to their definitions of leadership itself.

Many scholars have supported Rost's assertion that a reconceptualization of leadership theory must be made in response to the rapidly changing American society. In *The Leader of the Future*, from the Peter Drucker Foundation (Hesselbein et al., 1996), a collection of prominent leaders in both the private and public sectors contributes their thoughts and experiences on the future of leadership. Collectively, they identify globalization, diversity and social integration as forces shaping the future of leadership theory and development. The most marked result of these dynamics is the changing context of traditional hierarchical structures. Global interdependence has transformed the traditional hierarchy into a web of interdependent people (Lipman-Blumen, 1996). Essential to this process is the relationship between leading and following. "Leadership is now understood by many to imply collective action, orchestrated in such a way as to bring about significant change while raising the competencies and motivation of all those involved—that is, action where more than one individual influences the process" (Bornstein & Smith, 1996).

The new leadership models described by Rost and those scholars who contributed to *The Leader of the Future* were first exemplified by Greenleaf and Burns in the 1970s. Greenleaf's *The Servant as Leader* (1977) introduced the notion of servant leadership. This highly influential book juxtaposes the conventional notions of leadership and places the role of follower before the role of leader. In this approach, the servant leader is first a servant. Listening, understanding, language, imagination, acceptance and empathy form the central tenets of this theory (1977).

Burns, in his classic *Leadership* (1978) identified two types of leadership: transactional and transformational. According to Burns, transactional leadership describes the industrial models that draw a distinction between leaders and followers. In contrast, transformational leadership refers to a process in which an integral relationship between leader and follower is formed so that the motivation and morality of both parties are raised to a higher level (Northouse, 1997). In the mid-1980s, Bass extended this theoretical approach by describing transactional and transformational leadership as existing on a continuum, rather than being mutually independent (Northouse, 1997).

In their influential *Exploring Leadership: For College Students Who Want to Make a Difference*, Komives et al. (1998) articulate a vision of leadership as relational. This relational model of leadership builds on Stogdill's attentiveness to situations, but adds to this an element of Rost's prioritization of relationships between leaders and their community. For them, leadership is "a relational process of people together attempting to accomplish change or make a difference to benefit the common good" (Komives et al., 1998, p. 31). In their view, leadership is process-oriented, inclusive, empowering, purposeful, and ethical (Komives et al., p. 69).

Finally, the Social Change Model of Leadership (SCM), developed in the mid-1990s (Higher Education Research Institute [HERI], 1996), articulates a vision of non-hierarchical leadership as existing within three domains (the individual, group, and societal) and oriented toward change for the common good (see Bonous-Hammarth [Chapter 4 in this volume] for an overview of the SCM).

Rather than presenting a single, unified summary of the above-mentioned milestones in the development of the emerging post-industrial paradigm, it would be more useful to provide selected highlights from the work of the scholars noted above, as well as other theorists of leadership:

- Leadership is a relationship, not the property of an individual (Rogers, 1996);
- Leadership is a process (Northouse, 1997; Cherrey & Isgar, 1998);
- Leadership is about change (Rost, 1991);
- Leadership can be learned (Hesselbein et al., 1996);
- Leadership is inclusive (Rogers, 1996, p. 305);
- Leadership is collaborative (Rost, 1991; Northouse, 1997);
- Leadership is comprised of relationships (Komives et al., 1996);
- Leadership is oriented toward social change (HERI, 1996).

    In summary, our understanding of leadership has changed drastically over the course of the twentieth century. We have moved from the industrial notion that leadership is inherited by the few, to the emerging post-industrial imperative that everyone has inherited the mutual responsibility of leadership. It is only natural that our understanding of leadership education has evolved as well.

STUDENT LEADERSHIP DEVELOPMENT IN HIGHER EDUCATION

    The expressed intent for higher education to develop future leaders predates the history of leadership as a discipline by two hundred years. During the colonial era, *the* mission of higher education in the United States was to guarantee the preparation of a future leadership cohort (Thelin, 1996). Even as higher education developed and expanded, this objective has remained an important institutional goal; "Seldom do historic documents and emergent institutional missions neglect to laud the important purpose of developing leadership among students and graduates" (Roberts, 1997).

    While historians of higher education have no trouble documenting the fact that leadership development has always been a desired outcome of higher education, the means by which this has been achieved have been less clear. Until the twentieth century, leadership development was standard for all college students simply because higher education was reserved primarily for the elite. By social position alone, the majority of college graduates during the eighteenth and nineteenth centuries were destined to become some type of public leader. Thus, leadership "development" during this time can be understood more in terms of maintaining rather than gaining position (Thelin, 1996).

    As higher education diversified and evolved from a privilege of the elite to a right of the masses (Bowen, 1997), the objective of leadership development became diluted. The fact that leadership development does not fall within the domain of any single academic discipline may contribute to the lack of coherent leadership development programs in higher education (McIntire, 1989). Moreover, the intended outcome of civic leadership has become intertwined with the implicit assumption that educated individuals will practice leadership regardless of whether they were engaged in developmental activities during college (Roberts, 1997; Howe & Freeman, 1997).

The last 20 years have seen an increase in the number of leadership development programs in higher education. According to Roberts (1997), this movement was initiated in 1976 by the American College Personnel Association's (ACPA) Commission IV Leadership Task Force. Despite the increase in programs, few studies have attempted to examine or describe the context of contemporary leadership education systematically (Howe & Freeman, 1997).

A recent survey by the Center for Creative Leadership revealed the existence of 700 leadership development programs within higher education (Reisberg, 1998). The Center for Creative Leadership's *Leadership Education 1996–1997: A Source Book* (Freeman, Knott, & Schwartz, 1996) describes approximately 150 different courses and programs. These offerings span a broad spectrum of academic and co-curricular opportunities, from degree programs and courses to informal workshops. Courses are offered in an array of academic disciplines, from management to psychology, and programs are administered by both faculty and student affairs staff.

Scattered studies on the effects of these programs indicate mixed student development outcomes. Prola and Stern (1984) undertook a longitudinal analysis of elected student leaders at an urban institution who participated in a first-year orientation program with a goal of increasing academic and personal leadership. They found that a significantly higher proportion of student leaders participated in the first-year program than had not participated. They also found the program to have a significantly positive effect on persistence.

Astin's (1993) large-scale analysis of the impact of college sheds light on the factors related to leadership development. Astin's sample included two time points (1985, 1989) and was comprised of 24,847 students at 217 institutions. Leadership outcomes were measured by three self-rated items: leadership ability, popularity and social self-confidence, and election to a student leadership position. An increase in the aggregate score of the four leadership factors was interpreted as an increase in overall leadership.

Longitudinal analysis revealed that increases in leadership during college were associated with living on campus, the number of years of college completed, and the degree of student interaction with faculty. The strongest effect on increase in leadership rating was associated with interaction with peers. Students who frequently associated with peers showed the highest net increase in leadership. In contrast, students with the least amount of peer to peer interaction demonstrated a decrease in leadership over time.

In addition, leaving home to attend college was positively associated with leadership development, while engaging in outside (off-campus) work had a negative association with leadership. Interestingly, faculty research orientation was negatively associated with leadership development. Astin suggests that given the finding that faculty interaction was found to increase leadership, research orientation may be associated with less student to faculty interaction (p. 124).

Leadership increases were also associated with a variety of involvement factors, including membership in a fraternity or sorority, playing intramural sports, engaging in volunteer work, tutoring other students, participating in group projects in class, and making class presentations (p. 125).

While the aforementioned studies report the outcomes and factors associated with leadership development, none examine the specific intervention that may have caused the leadership development (although the first study briefly explains that participation in a first-year orientation program was the independent variable, it does not describe or analyze the elements of the program). Moreover, election to a student leadership position was used as the definition of student leader in each of the studies. While this is an indication of one type of leadership, it excludes students who, while not elected, may qualify as leaders. Examples of student leaders not elected to a position could include those who participate in service activities or independent research, or those who become resident advisors.

What becomes apparent from the lack of empirical studies on student leadership development is that while hundreds of documented leadership programs exist, researchers and administrators are not examining either the process or outcomes of these courses. See the chapters of Cress and Tyree [Chapters 22 and 23 in this volume] for more on the importance of assessing student leadership development.

SUMMARY

This overview of the emergence of the post-industrial leadership paradigm has provided a very brief summary of the current status of leadership theory and development in both the greater societal context and higher education. During the twentieth century, leadership theory in general has evolved from the one great leader approach to an emerging paradigm of inclusive leadership for the common good. This evolution has been paralleled by an equally significant opening of access to higher education, as our colleges and universities have shifted their missions from training the elite to educating a broader section of our society. As cultures combine, clash, and ultimately contribute to one another on our campuses, we can look to emerging collaborative models of leadership to point to new epistemologies in which the experience and contributions of all members of the learning community—from immigrant students to seasoned professors—are honored.

REFERENCES

Astin, A. W. (1993). *What matters in college? Four critical years revisited.* San Francisco: Jossey-Bass.

Bass, B. M. (1981). *Stogdill's handbook of leadership: A survey of theory and research.* New York: Free Press.

Bernard, L. L. (1926). *An introduction to social psychology.* New York: Holt.

Bird, C. (1940). *Social psychology.* New York: Appleton-Century.

Bornstein, S. M., & Smith, A. F. (1996). The puzzles of leadership. In F. Hesselbein, M. Goldsmith, & R. Beckhard (Eds.), *The leader of the future: New visions, strategies, and practices for the next era* (pp. 281–292). San Francisco: Jossey-Bass.

Bowen, H. (1997). *Investment in learning: The individual and social value of American higher education.* Baltimore: The Johns Hopkins University Press.

Burns, J. M. (1978). *Leadership.* New York: Harper & Row.

Cherrey, C., & Isgar, R. (1998). Leadership education in the context of the new millennium. *Concepts & Connections: A Newsletter for Leadership Educators, 6*(1), 5–11.

Freeman, F. H., Knott, K. B., & Schwartz, M. K. (Eds.). (1996). *Leadership education 1996–1997: A source book. Vol. 1: Courses and programs* (6th ed.). Greensboro, NC: Center for Creative Leadership.

Greenleaf, R. K. (1977). *The servant as leader: A journey into the nature of legitimate power and greatness.* New York: Paulist Press.

Hesselbein, F., Goldsmith, M., & Beckhard, R. (Eds.). (1996). *The leader of the future: New visions, strategies, and practices for the next era.* San Francisco: Jossey-Bass.

Higher Education Research Institute. (1996). *A Social Change Model of Leadership Development* (3rd ed.). Los Angeles: Author.

Howe, W., & Freeman, F. (1997). Leadership education in American colleges and universities: An overview. *Concepts & Connections: A Newsletter for Leadership Educators, 5*(2), 5–7.

Komives, S., Lucas, N., & McMahon, T. (1998). *Exploring leadership: For college students who want to make a difference.* San Francisco: Jossey-Bass.

Kuh, G. D. (1996). Organizational theory. In S. R. Komives & D. B. Woodard, Jr., et al. (Eds.), *Student services: A handbook for the profession* (3rd ed., pp. 269–294). San Francisco: Jossey-Bass.

Lipman-Blumen, J. (1996). *The connective edge: Leading in an interdependent world.* San Francisco: Jossey-Bass.

McIntire, D. D. (1989). Student leadership development: A student affairs mandate. *NASPA Journal, 27*(1), 74–79.

Northouse, P. G. (1997). *Leadership theory and practice.* Thousand Oaks, CA: Sage Publications.

Prola, M., & Stern, D. (1984, September). The effect of a freshman orientation program on student leadership and academic persistence. *Journal of College Student Personnel, 25,* 472–473.

Reisberg, L. (1998, October 30). Students gain sense of direction in new field of leadership studies. *Chronicle of Higher Education, 45,* A49.

Roberts, D. C. (1997). The changing look of leadership programs. *Concepts & Connections: A Newsletter for Leadership Educators, 5*(2), 1–7.

Rogers, J. L. (1996). Leadership. In S. R. Komives & D. B. Woodard, Jr., et al. (Eds.). *Student services: A handbook for the profession* (3rd ed., pp. 229–319). San Francisco: Jossey-Bass.

Rost, J. C. (1991). *Leadership for the twenty-first century.* New York: Praeger.

Rost, J. C. (1993). Leadership development for the new millennium. *Journal of Leadership Studies, 1*(1), 91–110.

Thelin, J. R. (1996). Historical overview of American higher education. In S. R. Komives & D. B. Woodard, Jr., et al. (Eds.), *Student services: A handbook for the profession* (3rd ed., pp. 22–42). San Francisco: Jossey-Bass.

Weber, M. (1947). *The theory of social and economic organizations.* New York: Free Press.

Chapter 3

A Multiple-Level Approach for Understanding the Nature of Leadership Studies

Francis J. Yammarino and Fred Dansereau

The *LQ* logo for the journal *Leadership Quarterly* contains the ancient Egyptian hieroglyphs for "leadership." So, for literally several thousand years, humankind has been writing about and trying to understand leadership. While there are numerous theories and models of leadership (for extensive reviews, see Bass, 1990; Dansereau & Yammarino, 1998a, 1998b; Yukl, 1998), it is useful to categorize them into four meta-approaches, all of which beginning with the letter "I"; hence, the *Four Is* of leadership. Likewise, while there are various ways to view human beings who comprise leadership systems (see Dansereau, Alutto, & Yammarino, 1984; Yammarino & Bass, 1991), four general perspectives or levels of analysis are useful to identify; hence the *Four Ls* (for levels of analysis) of leadership.

The purpose of this chapter is first to conceptualize the four meta-approaches to leadership—instrumental, inspirational, informal, and illusional—and the four general perspectives on human beings—persons, dyads, groups/teams, collectives/organizations/systems—and then integrate them into a "4 I by 4 L Leadership Matrix." The overall matrix approach is useful for summarizing the literature and categorizing leadership theories and models that are both hierarchical (i.e., based on levels of management) and non-hierarchical (i.e., based on flattening structures and prioritizing process over position) in nature. Next, focusing on the more comprehensive approaches within the matrix, a multiple-level model of leadership that includes the key variables from the meta-approaches and levels of analysis is articulated. This model can be viewed as a basis for future leadership research and studies. Finally, as a practical application of this multiple-level leadership model to the realm of higher education and student development, we describe briefly an existing three-course leadership concentration within the Masters of Business Administration program at the

Table 3.1
Four Is of Leadership

Instrumental Leadership
- Transactional
- Exchange
- Contingent Reward and Punishment

Inspirational Leadership
- Transformational
- Charismatic
- Visionary

Informal Leadership
- Elected
- Emergent
- Non-Appointed

Illusional Leadership
- Substitutes
- Implicit and Romantic
- Non-Contingent Reward and Punishment

State University of New York at Binghamton. We close with the implications of our overall approach for theory development, empirical testing, and professional practice in higher education and other arenas.

THE FOUR Is OF LEADERSHIP

Various theories, models, and substantive views of leadership can be identified in terms of four meta-approaches: instrumental, inspirational, informal, and illusional leadership. As summarized in Table 3.1, these terms are broad-based and integrative, each reflecting and encompassing many theories, models, and variables of leadership.

First I: Instrumental Leadership

Instrumental views of leadership involve a focus on transactions, exchanges, and contingent rewards and punishments (Bass, 1990; Dansereau & Yammarino,

1998a, 1998b; Yukl, 1998). Simply, exchanges or transactions are "tits for tats," "quid pro quos," or "you scratch my back and I'll scratch your back." Included in this category are many traditional and current views of leadership, such as the Ohio State work on consideration and initiating structure (Schriesheim & Kerr, 1977; Schriesheim, Cogliser, & Neider, 1998); Fiedler's contingency model (Fiedler, 1967; Ayman, Chemers, & Fiedler, 1998); House's path-goal theory (House, 1971, 1996); Podsakoff's contingent rewards and punishments work (Podsakoff & Schriesheim, 1985; Podsakoff & Todor, 1985; Podsakoff, Todor, & Skov, 1982); and Bass's (1985) and Burns's (1978) transactional leadership.

According to the instrumental view, if a follower provides high levels of performance, high levels of rewards should be forthcoming from a leader; if adequate performance is not provided, then no rewards, or perhaps punishments, will be forthcoming. So, rewards and punishments are contingent on, dependent on, and linked to performance. The exchanges or transactions of instrumental leadership may include both tangible (e.g., pay increases) and intangible (e.g., recognition) commodities. Leadership behaviors here include setting goals, coaching, and using incentives, showing consideration and being participatory, empowering, and delegating.

Second I: Inspirational Leadership

Inspirational views of leadership involve a focus on transformation, charisma, and the creation of visions (Bass, 1990; Cherrey & Isgar, 1998; Dansereau & Yammarino, 1998a, 1998b; Yukl, 1998). These theories and models tend to describe emotional and ideological appeals and change individuals' work values to consider the larger group (e.g., team, organization, society). Included in this category are many of the newer genre of leadership work, such as Bass's (1985) and Burns's (1978) transformational leadership, House's (1977; House, Spangler, & Woycke, 1991) charismatic leadership, Bryman's (1992) new models of leadership, the Social Change Model of Leadership (Higher Education Research Institute [HERI], 1996) and the relational leadership model (Komives, Lucas, & McMahon, 1998).

Simply, leadership here is more than mere exchanges of rewards for performance; exchanges form the base of leadership while inspiration augments the base. Typical leader behaviors include providing an inspirational vision, communicating confidence in followers, setting challenging performance expectations, providing individualized support to followers, being intellectually challenging and stimulating, recognizing accomplishments of followers, empowering others, and displaying exemplary actual and symbolic behaviors and actions. Inspirational leaders attempt to raise the needs of followers and promote the transformation of individuals, groups, organizations, and societies.

Third I: Informal Leadership

Informal views of leadership are those approaches that involve a focus on elected, emergent, and non-appointed leaders (Bass, 1990; Yukl, 1998). These theories and models tend to describe individual contributions to group/team goals, work facilitation of others, and offering support, direction, and collaboration with coworkers or team members. Included in this category is much work in small group settings, especially the work of Hollander and his colleagues (1958, 1978, 1985, 1992) and other non-hierarchical leadership approaches (e.g., Cherrey & Isgar, 1998; HERI, 1996; Komives et al., 1998).

Informal leadership, although associated often with non-organizational settings, occurs within organizations as well as in small groups and informal groups. Leader emergence, in contrast to leadership per se, is always a result of social interaction and consensus among members of a group or team that a particular individual can "lead" the group to attain group goals. Simply, an individual group member becomes elevated to a position of status and leadership, often without corresponding formal title or appointment. Informal leaders tend to adapt their style of performance and leadership to the needs of the group or team.

Fourth I: Illusional Leadership

Illusional views of leadership involve a focus on substitutes for leadership, implicit leadership, and non-contingent rewards and punishments (Bass, 1990; Yukl, 1998). These theories and models tend to view leadership as an illusion or as illusive, attributing behavior, actions, and performance to leadership when none may exist. Included in this category are approaches such as Kerr and Jermier's (1978) substitutes for leadership, Meindl's (1998) romance of leadership, the implicit and information-processing views of Lord and his colleagues (Hall & Lord, 1998; Lord, Foti, & DeVader, 1984), random acts of non-contingent (non-instrumental) rewarding and punishing (Podsakoff & Todor, 1985; Podsakoff et al., 1982), and at an extreme, the complete abdication of leadership called laissez-faire leadership (Bass, 1985, 1990).

In the illusional view, the functions served by leaders for their followers may be accomplished by means other than the leaders' behavior. Such substitutes for leadership may be real, such as followers' knowledge, skills, and abilities or an organization's rules, regulations, and procedures; or they may be symbolic, illusory, or romantic phenomena. A related view is that leadership is implicit in nature and based on individuals' processing of information. Leaders and followers see things differently and respond differently based on their own preconceptions, perceptions, and attributions; or leadership can become a romantic notion, and individuals attribute good and bad events to leadership.

Table 3.2
Four Ls of Leadership

Person Level of Analysis
• Independent Human Beings
• Individual Differences
• Individual Employees
  —Leader or Follower

Dyad Level of Analysis
• One-to-One Interdependence
• Interpersonal Relationships
• Two-Person Group or Team
  —Leader-Follower Relationship

Group/Team Level of Analysis
• Face-to-Face Interdependence
• Group/Team Dynamics
• Three or More Persons/Multiple Dyads
  —Leader-Group Interaction

Collective/Organization/System Level of Analysis
• Interdependence via Shared Expectations
• Systems and Subsystems
• Groups of Groups/Echelons

THE FOUR Ls OF LEADERSHIP

Various perspectives on human beings are called "levels of analysis." As summarized in Table 3.2, the levels (Ls) relevant for leadership include persons, dyads, groups/teams, and collectives, which include organizations and larger social systems. These levels of analysis are non-hierarchical (i.e., not based on levels of management or hierarchies), and they can be viewed as different "lenses" through which to view the individuals who comprise groups, organizations, and societies (Dansereau, Alutto, & Yammarino, 1984; Dansereau & Yammarino, 1998a, 1998b; Yammarino & Bass, 1991).

First L: Person Level of Analysis

Individuals who comprise a group, organization, or society can be viewed as persons, independent of one another. Persons display various individual differences in knowledge, skills, abilities, personality, and so forth. From one perspective, leaders can be viewed as unique persons; from another perspective, followers can be viewed as independent persons.

Second L: Dyad Level of Analysis

Individuals can be viewed as dyads, interdependent on a one-to-one basis. Dyads are two-person groups and are very important in society. Consider, for example, the key roles played by the following dyads: husband-wife, significant others, best friends, parent-child, and so on. Likewise, dyads are particularly important in organizations because organizations are often viewed as being built through superior-subordinate (leader-follower) dyads. The interpersonal relationships in organizations, whether leader-follower or coworker-coworker, are critical for determining what gets accomplished.

Third L: Group/Team Level of Analysis

Individuals who comprise an organization or society can be viewed as groups or several individuals who are interdependent and interact on a face-to-face basis. They also can be linked via various technologies (e.g., computers, fax machines, teleconference equipment) in virtual groups or teams. In organizations, a work group or team can be identified often as those individuals who report to a common, immediate superior; however, there may be a lack of hierarchy in teams. Various social, non-work groups and teams are also relevant.

Fourth L: Collective Level of Analysis

Individuals can be viewed as collectives or groups of groups (individuals) who are interdependent based on a set of shared expectations. Collectives may be systems (e.g., production, support, managerial) or subsystems (e.g., functional areas, departments) of the organization, the entire organization, a part of a society, or the society itself. These collectives are typically held together by echelons and identified by various "titles" or names. For example, saying you are a member of the company "production department," or the university "athletic department," or the "XYZ Corporation," or the "ABC Social Movement," conjures up images and expectations that you hold in common with other members of that collective, even those you may not know personally. Nevertheless, you typically share a common heritage, work on related tasks, endorse similar values and beliefs, and follow similar procedures.

A LEADERSHIP MATRIX: 4 Is BY 4 Ls

By combining the Four Is with the Four Ls, it is possible to describe a leadership matrix for understanding leadership in organizations and society. By also considering how leadership and levels of analysis may change over time in terms

Figure 3.1
A Multiple-Level Multidimensional Model of Leadership

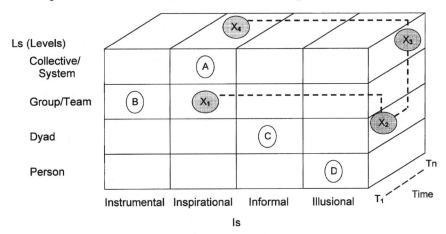

Source: Adapted from Dansereau & Yammarino (1998b), p. 329.

of the Is and the Ls (Dansereau, Yammarino, & Kohles, 1999), a more complete matrix can be created with "Time" as a third dimension. As shown in Figure 3.1, instrumental, inspirational, informal, and illusional leadership can be conceived as operating via persons, dyads, groups/teams, and collectives/systems and as changing over time.

The I by L by Time Leadership Matrix is a useful heuristic device for classifying past and current leadership research and for identifying future leadership studies. This extended matrix may be useful also for practicing managers, professionals, and educators as they try to understand leadership and its implications. For example, the chief executive setting the vision for the organization that all groups buy into can be viewed as collective-level inspirational leadership—Cell A in the matrix (Waldman & Yammarino, 1999). The head of a social movement articulating a mission with which all members identify is a similar example. In contrast, team leaders enforcing safety regulations across all team members to generate adequate and safe performance is an example of group-level instrumental leadership—Cell B in the matrix. The computer expert on a project team who has no official title, yet goes out of his/her way to help each individual on the team, one on one, is displaying dyad-level informal leadership—Cell C in the matrix. Individuals, whether leaders or followers, who accomplish things based on their individual talents without direction or guidance is an example of person-level illusional leadership—Cell D in the matrix. As outsiders, we may think or perceive the results to be due to leadership when in fact they are due to individuals' differential skills and abilities, regardless of leadership. This can occur in athletics, for example, where individual physical talents are often confused with or labeled leadership, when in fact they are not.

Over time, different types of leadership and levels of analysis may manifest themselves in organizations and society. For example, relationships may start out at a group level (cell X_1 in Figure 3.1). Stronger relationships develop with some but not all followers. These relationships are managed by the leader. Relationships may then develop, after another period of time, to the point where they are independent of the group and based in dyads (cell X_2 in Figure 3.1). Leaders and followers link independently of the groups, there is sharing and mutual control, and they reach agreement or consensus on each of these one-to-one relationships (dyads); some relationships are "rich" while others are "poor." These dyadic relationships could then serve as the basis for integrating entire groups, teams, or collectives (cells X_3 and X_4 in Figure 3.1). Clearly, there are many other possible scenarios.

A MULTIPLE-LEVEL MODEL OF LEADERSHIP

Another way to use the leadership matrix is to view leadership as a multiple-level phenomena (Dansereau et al., 1984; Dansereau & Yammarino, 1998a, 1998b; Dansereau, Yammarino & Markham, 1995; Yammarino & Bass, 1991). In Figure 3.2, one multiple-level, multidimensional leadership model is presented (Dansereau & Yammarino, 1998b).

This leadership model consists of five key areas of research focus:

1. *fundamental human processes*—those notions linked most directly to foundation areas in psychology and related fields;
2. *leadership core processes*—those notions described above as examples of leadership in terms of the person, dyad, group/team, and collective/system levels;
3. *leadership outcomes*—key "dependent variables" or first-level outcomes for leadership researchers;
4. *other multi-level outcomes*—traditional "dependent variables" or second-level outcomes for scholars in the field; and
5. *substitutes for leadership*—alternative elements and processes that may replace, neutralize, or enhance the effects of leadership in organizations and society.

Fundamental Human Processes

A set of psychological and related processes focus on explaining the fundamental or underlying reasons about why human beings develop relationships that people think of as leadership. These include notions such as affective and cognitive processes at the individual level (Hall & Lord, 1998), interpersonal attraction and exchange processes at the dyad level (Dansereau, Yammarino, Markham et al., 1998; Hall & Lord, 1998), climate and norms at the group or team level (Meindl, 1998), and various collective-level factors such as societal culture and values and organizational variables (Hunt & Ropo, 1998). Finally, cutting across levels of analysis is communication, a multiple-level process.

Figure 3.2
A Multiple-Level Multidimensional Model of Leadership

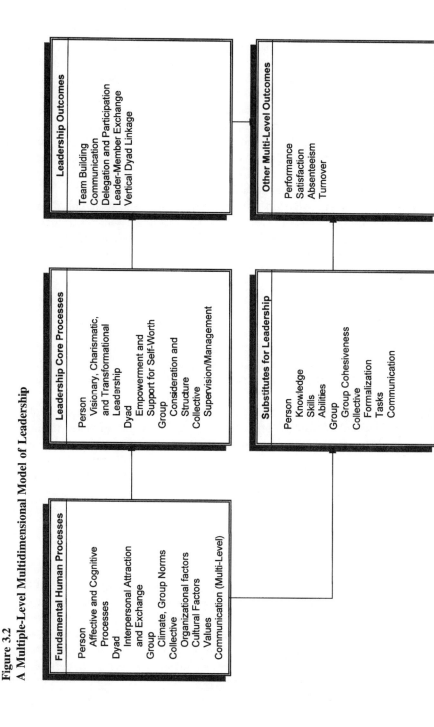

Source: Adapted from Dansereau & Yammarino (1998b), p. 329.

Core Leadership Processes

There are several core leadership approaches. The first, a person-level process, includes charisma and transformational leadership—the inspirational (second I) dimension—because in theory these refer to the characteristics of the leader as a person (Avolio & Bass, 1998; Klein & House, 1998). The second process involves the dyadic exchanges between leaders and followers, which is referred to as individualized leadership or empowerment (Dansereau, Yammarino, Markham et al., 1998). This has elements of both the instrumental and informal dimensions (first and third Is). The third addresses group dynamics and the degree to which leaders provide task and relationship functions to their groups or teams (Ayman et al., 1998; Kim & Yukl, 1998; Schriesheim et al., 1998)— instrumental (first I) leadership. The last process refers to hierarchical supervision or management, which is defined as the ability to function in a (formal) role system (Hunt & Ropo, 1998; Kim & Yukl, 1998). In other words, included as part of this notion is the ability of leaders to understand rules, regulations, and procedures and to change them as may be appropriate.

Leadership Outcomes

Other approaches attempt to include multiple levels of analysis as first-level leadership "outcomes." For example, the notion of team building (Markham & Markham, 1998) suggests that leaders as persons should behave in ways that empower individuals (dyadic-level effect) and, at the same time, allow group functions (tasks and relationships) to be performed. In addition, team building seems to imply the existence of a formal system (the core of supervision) that requires superiors to behave in a particular team-oriented way. Approaches in this category include participation in decision making (Vroom & Jago, 1998), leader-member exchange theory (Graen & Uhl-Bien, 1998), and the vertical dyad linkage approach to in-group and out-group members (Dansereau et al., 1984, 1995).

Other Multi-Level Outcomes

Various other second-level outcomes include performance (quantity and quality), satisfaction, absenteeism, and turnover, which can be defined in several ways and at each of several levels of analysis (Bass, 1990; Yukl, 1998). For example, one can conceive of an individual as being very effective (person level) but as a part of a poorly performing team or group contained within a highly successful organization or social movement (collective level). Thus, performance can be viewed at different levels of analysis.

Substitutes for Leadership

In addition to leadership, the multi-level (secondary) outcomes may also be due to substitutes for leadership—the illusional (fourth I) dimension (Podsakoff & MacKenzie, 1998). Serving as enhancements to, neutralizers of, or replacements for the leadership core processes and (first-level) leadership outcomes, substitutes for leadership include at least: the knowledge and skills of individuals (person level), group or team cohesiveness, and various collective-level variables such as organizational formalization, task design, and communication systems. In other words, they are inherent in non-hierarchical leadership (i.e., based on levels of analysis rather than levels of management).

Linking the Pieces Together

As shown in the integrative model in Figure 3.2, fundamental human processes or capabilities underlie various leadership and other substitute processes, which in turn produce various leadership and multi-level outcomes. Within this overall view, the pieces can be moved around in a variety of ways. Thus, the arrows in Figure 3.2 are not meant to show direct causation, but rather indicate that one set of factors influences another set. Moreover, even though the arrows have direction, this does not imply that, from a temporal perspective, variables cannot operate in reverse.

THREE-COURSE LEADERSHIP CONCENTRATION

As a practical application of this overall multiple-level model of leadership to the higher education realm, we have created a three-course leadership concentration within the Masters of Business Administration (MBA) program at the State University of New York at Binghamton. Course 1 is offered in the fall semester, and Courses 2 and 3 occur in the spring semester. The concentration, offered through the Center for Leadership Studies, serves as a "major" for students in the MBA program.

Course 1, *Individual Leadership*, focuses on the first L—person level—and all four Is of leadership, the fundamental human processes, and the person-level leadership core and substitute processes from the multiple-level model. Course 2, *Team Leadership*, involves the second and third Ls—dyad and group/team levels—and all four Is of leadership, and the dyad- and group-level leadership core and substitute processes. Course 3, *Strategic Leadership*, focuses on the fourth L—collective level—and all four Is of leadership and the collective-level leadership core and substitute processes. All three courses include a specific examination of the leadership and other multi-level outcomes from the integration model.

The three courses focus on both formal organizations and non-organizational settings, and use a variety of pedagogical techniques. Mini-lectures on the various topics are supplemented by discussions, cases, experiential exercises, various individual assessments and feedback, several team projects and presentations, and virtual classes that include e-mail, on-line chats, and web-board sessions. The objective in all instances is to better understand the Is and Ls of leadership from an integrative multiple-level perspective. As there has been considerable interest in these three leadership courses across the university and the business communities, plans are underway to offer the sequence at the undergraduate level for both business and non-business (e.g., liberal arts) majors as well as on an "executive" basis for full-time working professionals.

IMPLICATIONS AND CONCLUSION

This multiple-level approach for leadership studies has some implications for theory formulation, empirical testing, and professional practice. In terms of theory formulation, the development and extension of current and future theories and models of instrumental, inspirational, informal, and illusional leadership could benefit from an explicit consideration of multiple levels of analysis. By "pushing" each theoretical formulation to incorporate levels of analysis in a specific manner, clarification of the theories and models occurs and new propositions and hypotheses for testing are generated. This approach also permits the identification of commonalities across theories and models of leadership. Such commonalities may move the field closer to an integrative and comprehensive theory of leadership.

After clarifying and formulating theories of leadership, the research process must move to the realm of testing the propositions and hypotheses that have been generated. If the approach presented here is viewed as a set of integrated propositions about instrumental, inspirational, informal, and illusional leadership *and* levels of analysis, then, through a series of studies, it could be subjected to empirical tests.

In terms of professional practice, whether in higher education or other realms, professionals need to avoid assuming that there is one best way to lead (Cherry & Isgar, 1998; HERI, 1996; Komives et al., 1998). Regardless of the issues involved (e.g., diagnosis of whether ability, training, or motivational increases are needed for improvements, or whether resources and facilities changes are needed), multiple levels of analysis are an important concern for practicing professionals. Thus, multiple levels of analysis issues should be of concern in policy formulation and implementation.

In short, whether the focus is on theory building, empirical testing, or professional practice; whether instrumental, inspirational, informal or illusional approaches are involved; whether based on persons, dyads, groups/teams, or collectives/systems; whether a single-level focus or an integrative, multiple-level approach; *leadership* is the key for student development and managerial, professional, and educational success and effectiveness.

REFERENCES

Avolio, B. J., & Bass, B. M. (1998). Individual consideration viewed at multiple levels of analysis: A multi-level framework for examining the diffusion of transformational leadership. In F. Dansereau & F. J. Yammarino (Eds.), *Leadership: The multiple-level approaches (Part B: Contemporary and alternative)* (pp. 53–76). Stamford, CT: JAI Press.

Ayman, R., Chemers, M. M., & Fiedler, F. (1998). The contingency model of leadership effectiveness: Its levels of analysis. In F. Dansereau & F. J. Yammarino (Eds.), *Leadership: The multiple-level approaches (Part A: Classical and new wave)* (pp. 73–113). Stamford, CT: JAI Press.

Bass, B. M. (1985). *Leadership and performance beyond expectations.* New York: Free Press.

Bass, B. M. (1990). *Bass & Stogdill's handbook of leadership.* New York: Free Press.

Burns, J. M. (1978). *Leadership.* New York: Harper & Row.

Bryman, A. (1992). *Charisma and leadership in organizations.* London: Sage.

Cherrey, C., & Isgar, R. (1998). Leadership education in the context of the new millennium. *Concepts & Connections: A Newsletter for Leadership Educators, 6*(1), 5–11.

Dansereau, F., Alutto, J. A., & Yammarino, F. J. (1984). *Theory testing in organizational behavior: The variant approach.* Englewood Cliffs, NJ: Prentice-Hall.

Dansereau, F., & Yammarino, F. J. (Eds.) (1998a). *Leadership: The multiple-level approaches (Part A: Classical and new wave).* Stamford, CT: JAI Press.

Dansereau, F., & Yammarino, F. J. (Eds.) (1998b). *Leadership: The multiple-level approaches (Part B: Contemporary and alternative).* Stamford, CT: JAI Press.

Dansereau, F., Yammarino, F. J., & Kohles, J. C. (1999). Multiple levels of analysis from a longitudinal perspective: Some implications for theory building. *Academy of Management Review, 24,* 346–357.

Dansereau, F., Yammarino, F. J., & Markham, S. E. (1995). Leadership: The multiple-level approaches. *Leadership Quarterly, 6,* 251–263.

Dansereau, F., Yammarino, F. J., Markham, S. E., Alutto, J. A., Newman, J., Dumas, M., Nachman, S. A., Naughton, T. J., Kim, K., Al-Kelabi, S. A., Lee, S., & Keller, T. (1998). Individualized leadership: A new multiple-level approach. In F. Dansereau & F. J. Yammarino (Eds.), *Leadership: The multiple-level approaches (Part A: Classical and new wave)* (pp. 363–410). Stamford, CT: JAI Press.

Fiedler, F. E. (1967). *A theory of leadership effectiveness.* New York: McGraw-Hill.

Graen, G., & Uhl-Bien, M. (1998). Relationship-based approach to leadership: Development of leader-member exchange (LMX) theory of leadership over 25 years: Applying a multilevel multi-domain perspective. In F. Dansereau & F. J. Yammarino (Eds.), *Leadership: The multiple-level approaches (Part B: Contemporary and alternative)* (pp. 103–133). Stamford, CT: JAI Press.

Hall, R. J., & Lord, R. G. (1998). Multi-level information-processing explanations of followers' leadership perceptions. In F. Dansereau & F. J. Yammarino (Eds.), *Leadership: The multiple-level approaches (Part B: Contemporary and alternative)* (pp. 159–190). Stamford, CT: JAI Press.

Higher Education Research Institute. (1996). *A Social Change Model of Leadership Development* (3rd ed.). Los Angeles: Author.

Hollander, E. P. (1958). Conformity, status, and idiosyncrasy credit. *Psychological Review, 65,* 117–127.

Hollander, E. P. (1978). *Leadership dynamics.* New York: Free Press.

Hollander, E. P. (1985). Leadership and power. In G. Lindsey & E. Aronson (Eds.), *The handbook of social psychology* (pp. 485–537). New York: Random House.

Hollander, E. P. (1992). Leadership, followership, self, and others. *Leadership Quarterly, 3,* 43–54.

House, R. J. (1971). A path-goal theory of leadership effectiveness. *Administrative Science Quarterly, 16,* 321–338.

House, R. J. (1977). A 1976 theory of charismatic leadership. In J. G. Hunt & L. L. Larson (Eds.), *Leadership: The cutting edge* (pp. 194–205). Carbondale, IL: Southern Illinois University Press.

House, R. J. (1996). Path-goal theory of leadership: Lessons, legacy, and a reformulated theory. *Leadership Quarterly, 7,* 323–352.

House, R. J., Spangler, W. D., & Woycke, J. (1991). Personality and charisma in the US presidency: A psychological theory of leadership effectiveness. *Administrative Science Quarterly, 36,* 364–396.

Hunt, J. G., & Ropo, A. (1998). Multi-level leadership: Grounded theory and mainstream theory applied to the case of General Motors. In F. Dansereau & F. J. Yammarino (Eds.), *Leadership: The multiple-level approaches (Part A: Classical and new wave)* (pp. 289–340). Stamford, CT: JAI Press.

Kerr, S., & Jermier, J. M. (1978). Substitutes for leadership: Their meaning and measurement. *Organizational Behavior and Human Performance, 22,* 375–403.

Kim, H., & Yukl, G. A. (1998). Relationships of managerial effectiveness and advancement to self-reported and subordinate-reported leadership behaviors from the multiple-linkage model. In F. Dansereau & F. J. Yammarino (Eds.), *Leadership: The multiple-level approaches (Part A: Classical and new wave)* (pp. 243–264). Stamford, CT: JAI Press.

Klein, K. J., & House, R. J. (1998). On fire: Charismatic leadership and levels of analysis. In F. Dansereau & F. J. Yammarino (Eds.), *Leadership: The multiple-level approaches (Part B: Contemporary and alternative)* (pp. 3–29). Stamford, CT: JAI Press.

Komives, S. R., Lucas, N., & McMahon, T. R. (1998). *Exploring leadership: For college students who want to make a difference.* San Francisco: Jossey-Bass.

Lord, R. G., Foti, R. J., & DeVader, C. L. (1984). A test of leadership categorization theory: Internal structure, information processing and leadership perceptions. *Organizational Behavior and Human Performance, 34,* 343–378.

Markham, S. E., & Markham, I. S. (1998). Self-management and self-leadership reexamined: A levels-of-analysis perspective. In F. Dansereau & F. J. Yammarino (Eds.), *Leadership: The multiple-level approaches (Part A: Classical and new wave)* (pp. 193–212). Stamford, CT: JAI Press.

Meindl, J. R. (1998). The romance of leadership as a follower-centric theory: A social constructionist approach. In F. Dansereau & F. J. Yammarino (Eds.), *Leadership: The multiple-level approaches (Part B: Contemporary and alternative)* (pp. 285–301). Stamford, CT: JAI Press.

Podsakoff, P. M., & MacKenzie, S. B. (1998). An examination of substitutes for leadership within a levels-of-analysis framework. In F. Dansereau & F. J. Yammarino

(Eds.), *Leadership: The multiple-level approaches (Part B: Contemporary and alternative)* (pp. 215–260). Stamford, CT: JAI Press.

Podsakoff, P. M., & Schriesheim, C. A. (1985). *Leader reward and punishment behavior: A methodological and substantive review.* Bloomington, IN: Working Paper, Graduate School of Business, Indiana University.

Podsakoff, P. M., & Todor, W. D. (1985). Relationships between leader reward and punishment behavior and group processes and productivity. *Journal of Management, 11*, 55–73.

Podsakoff, P. M., Todor, W. D., & Skov, R. (1982). Effects of leader contingent satisfaction. *Academy of Management Journal, 25*, 810–821.

Schriesheim, C. A., Cogliser, C. C., & Neider, L. L. (1998). Is it "trustworthy"? A multiple-levels-of-analysis reexamination of an Ohio State leadership study, with implications for future research. In F. Dansereau & F. J. Yammarino (Eds.), *Leadership: The multiple-level approaches (Part A: Classical and new wave)* (pp. 3–50). Stamford, CT: JAI Press.

Schriesheim, C. A., & Kerr, S. (1977). Theories and measures of leadership: A critical appraisal of current and future directions. In J. G. Hunt & L. L. Larson (Eds.), *Leadership: The cutting edge* (pp. 9–45). Carbondale, IL: Southern Illinois University Press.

Vroom, V. H., & Jago, A. G. (1998). Situation effects and levels of analysis in the study of leader participation. In F. Dansereau & F. J. Yammarino (Eds.), *Leadership: The multiple-level approaches (Part A: Classical and new wave)* (pp. 145–161). Stamford, CT: JAI Press.

Waldman, D. A., & Yammarino, F. J. (1999). CEO charismatic leadership: Levels of management and levels of analysis effects. *Academy of Management Review, 24*, 266–285.

Yammarino, F. J., & Bass, B. M. (1991). Person and situation views of leadership: A multiple levels of analysis approach. *Leadership Quarterly, 2*, 121–139.

Yukl, G. A. (1998). *Leadership in organizations.* Englewood Cliffs, NJ: Prentice-Hall.

Chapter 4

Developing Social Change Agents: Leadership Development for the 1990s and Beyond

Marguerite Bonous-Hammarth

What's happened to leadership today? Whether we're reading Hillary Clinton's (1996) thoughts on the quality of life for children or David Putnam's (1995) ideas about declining civic involvement among Americans, we cannot escape the inverse parallel between the increasing social problems we face and the decreasing activism and effectiveness among people to collaboratively resolve these issues. As many other public opinionists have shown, as a society we seem less willing to take the time to make a difference in our communities— evidenced by declining participation in voting and in such memberships as labor unions, PTAs, and the Red Cross. For social researchers such as Putnam, the most unsettling sign of this disengagement is that Americans are bowling more than they did a decade ago but are joining bowling leagues and other organized clubs less. What this trend says about civic engagement and the future of democracy points us to the need to motivate individuals to develop their talents and to invest their energies in activities on behalf of our communities.

ENSEMBLING IDEAS ON LEADERSHIP

Developing essential leadership skills among diverse people in our society may be easier said than done. However, one very committed group of individuals met for two years to discuss such strategies. We called ourselves simply "the Ensemble," using the musical metaphor to describe our belief that our success resulted from the combined talents and efforts of each member. Our discussions were made possible by funding from the Eisenhower Leadership Program of the U.S. Department of Education and by coordination provided by the Higher Education Research Institute at the University of California, Los

Angeles. (Helen and Alexander Astin served as co-principal investigators for the project.)

During our discussions, we entered into a process of discovery ourselves. The path led us first to understand the values and world-view required of individuals who would be "social change agents," resolving problems that had lasting impact on our society. We then mapped out the process by which individuals could positively contribute to such efforts, which we referred to as "a Social Change Model of Leadership Development (SCM)" (Higher Education Research Institute, UCLA, 1996). The SCM provides a framework for understanding the different levels of interaction among individuals which foster leadership development. At an individual level, there are personal qualities which support and enhance group functioning and make social change possible. At a group level, there are ways individuals collaborate which enhance their own qualities and the qualities of others while impacting change. At the community/society level, leadership activities can be directed to address social concerns, and these service activities can nurture individual qualities and group interactions.

It goes without saying that our Ensemble members brought with them very diverse skills and a wealth of information on research in the field. Our initial ideas about leadership were guided by three particular studies, respectively conducted by Astin and Scherrei (1980), Astin (1993) and Astin and Leland (1991). Astin and Scherrei (1980) examined the influence of particular leadership styles on faculty and college outcomes and found that positive outcomes among faculty and students were associated with institutional leaders who were egalitarian (rather than bureaucratic) in their leadership approaches and whose overall administrative style was characterized as humanistic rather than hierarchical. Conversely, the most negative outcomes were associated with hierarchical administrations and bureaucratic leadership styles. Additionally, the longitudinal research by Astin (1993) suggests that the peer group—and specifically the amount of interaction that students have with each other—is one of the most potent sources of influence on leadership development. Lastly, Astin and Leland (1991) suggested that effective leadership involved collective action, shared power, and a passionate commitment to social justice ideals. The "leaders" in their study were self-aware, trusted others, did their homework, and listened to and empowered others.

These studies and other empirical work in the field reinforced our own ideas, beliefs and knowledge about the importance of collaboration and of developing the self as essential first steps to enhance group interactions (see, for example *Leadership for the Common Good* [Bryson and Crosby, 1992]; *Stewardship: Choosing Service over Self-Interest* [Block, 1993]; and *The Leader Within*, [Haas, 1992]). Thus, the SCM serves as a vehicle for leadership development by emphasizing clarification of values, development of self-awareness, ability to build trust, capacity to listen and serve others, collaborative work, and change for the common good.

Before sharing this model, it is important to note that our Ensemble discussed leadership as a process or way of channeling skills and energies to some ultimate purpose—that of contributing to the society and social outcomes. Providing service is a means to develop leadership skills. To this end, we believe that it is possible for all individuals to be leaders, to develop leadership skills, and to make a difference in society.

Our idea of leadership also is based on values, which we believe promote more effective interpersonal interactions to benefit the common good. In this sense, leadership is not divisive, biased, or authoritarian, but inclusive and focused on individual, group, and societal/community values.

THE SEVEN Cs OF CHANGE

Seven basic values, referred to as the Seven Cs of Change, comprise our model, emphasizing individual, group, and community aspects of leadership, which we believe revolve around a hub: *Change.*

Consciousness of self, congruence, and *commitment* comprise the individual values. Individual values are ones that an individual strives to develop and exhibit during the group process of leadership.

Consciousness of self means to be aware of self, knowing the values, emotions, attitudes, and beliefs that motivate the self to take action. Knowing one's self is a fundamental skill required to understand others and to understand how best one can contribute to a group effort.

Congruence refers to thinking, feeling and behaving with consistency, authenticity, and honesty toward others. Congruent persons are those whose actions are consistent with their most deeply-held beliefs and convictions.

Commitment is the energy that motivates the individual to serve and that drives the collective effort. Commitment implies passion, intensity, and duration. Without commitment, knowledge of self is of little value. And without knowledge of self, commitment is easily misdirected. Congruence, in turn, is most readily achieved when the person acts with commitment and knowledge of self.

In addition to these individual values, *collaboration, common purpose,* and *controversy with civility* comprise the group values. Group values are those that are expressed and practiced in the group work of the leadership process.

Collaboration, as mentioned earlier, is central to viewing leadership as a group process. This value characterizes the relational aspects in the model. Leadership involves human relationships and interactions to accomplish service. Collaboration involves working together toward common goals by sharing responsibility and accountability in achieving these goals. Collaboration promotes group effectiveness because it capitalizes on the diverse talents and perspectives of each group member and the power of that diversity to generate creative solutions to issues affecting the community or the society at large.

Common purpose refers to the work one does with others framed within a shared set of aims and values. Having these shared aims facilitates the group's

Figure 4.1
The Three Domains of the Social Change Model of Leadership Development

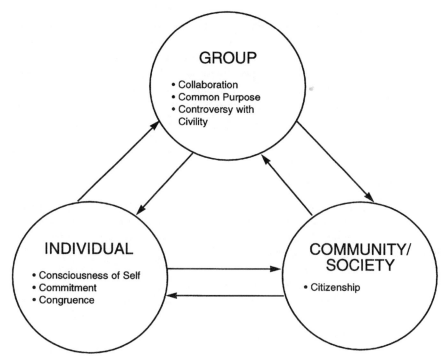

Source: Adapted from Bonous-Hammarth (1996).

ability to engage in collective analyses of the issues and the task to be under-taken.

Controversy with civility recognizes two fundamental realities of group inter-actions: that differences in viewpoint are inevitable and valuable and that such differences must be aired openly and with civility. Disagreements and differ-ences can be resolved through open and honest dialogue with the group's com-mitment to understand the sources of the disagreement and to work cooperatively toward common solutions.

The last value in the model, *citizenship*, describes the process whereby the self is responsibly connected to the environment and the community. Citizenship refers to more than membership in a democratic community, but it implies active engagement of the individual and the leadership group in an effort to serve the community. It implies social or civic responsibility—a concern with and caring for others. As seen in Figure 4.1, these values interact with one another, con-tinually influencing and being influenced by other individual and group values.

A SOCIAL CHANGE MODEL OF LEADERSHIP DEVELOPMENT

Thus, our leadership model seeks to develop a *conscious* and *congruent* person who can *collaborate* with others, who can become a *committed* participant in the shaping of the group's *common purpose*, who can help to resolve *controversy with civility* and be a responsible *citizen*. In sketching out this framework for discussion, we recognize that ours is but one model available for educators to consider. Although the basic aspects of the model, its values, are discussed here, the way these values shape our leaders for the future continues to evolve.

Applying the Social Change Model

Our model can be adopted in leadership education efforts and has been used with undergraduate and graduate students throughout the nation. In addition, St. Norbert's College has developed an applications guidebook based on the model (*Leadership for the New Millennium* by Knobloch, 1996). While our initial discussions centered on how the SCM could be applied in developing the leadership talents of undergraduate college students, we believe the model is an appropriate tool for designing programs to train the trainers and other professionals. However, there are some essential features that need to be considered in designing the leadership project. Specifically, one has to consider:

- The physical setting where one can initiate a leadership project (e.g., residence halls, classrooms, work environments, community sites).
- Preliminary task definition. What is the need or problem? What changes are needed?
- Involvement of participants: Identification of personal and shared values; discussion and shared perception of need.
- Task research/redefinition: Gathering of information about the task or need.
- Division of labor: What skills or knowledge are needed? Which members of the leadership group have the knowledge or skills? How do you acquire what knowledge or skills are needed? Each participant assumes a role or responsibility in the project.
- Mode of group functioning: Debriefing, reflection, and feedback are essential group activities. The leadership group meets regularly and processes the group activities. Openness, honesty, and sensitivity in providing critical feedback where needed are emphasized. The members of the group work on values clarification, increased self-knowledge, and group facilitation skills.

In *An American Imperative* (1993), Wingspread Group members issued a call for institutions of higher education to take actions to ensure that future generations of students would graduate with increased abilities to positively contribute to society and to further ideals of civility. Our Ensemble took these appeals to heart and developed a model, which we believe can foster leadership skills in each individual and ultimately refocus our attention to resolving social issues more effectively.

None of the Ensemble's efforts occurred in a vacuum. We are indebted to the professionals and various professional associations who provided our Ensemble with feedback and suggestions on how the SCM could be applied to educate youth, train practitioners, and impact social change. As more educators use the SCM at their institutions, we look forward to extending the discussion on leadership development by adding their stories of success and challenge. There remains much work to do and, fortunately, many change agents committed to these efforts.

NOTES

This chapter first appeared (in a slightly different form) in *Concepts & Connections* as "Developing social change agents: Leadership development for the '90s and beyond," *Concepts and Connections, 4*(2), 1–4. Reprinted with permission.

This chapter is based on the ideas generated by the collective efforts of A. W. Astin, Helen S. Astin, KC Boatsman, Marguerite Bonous-Hammarth, Tony Chambers, Leonard Goldberg, Cynthia Johnson, Susan Komives, Emily Langdon, Carole Leland, Nance Lucas, Raechele Pope, Dennis Roberts, Kathy Shellogg and Lisa Tsui.

REFERENCES

Astin, A. W. (1993). *What matters in college? Four critical years revisited.* San Francisco: Jossey-Bass.

Astin, A. W., & Scherrei, R. A. (1980). *Maximizing leadership effectiveness.* San Francisco: Jossey-Bass.

Astin, H. S., & Leland, C. (1991). *Women of influence, women of vision: A cross-generational study of leaders and social change.* San Francisco: Jossey-Bass.

Block, P. (1993). *Stewardship: Choosing service over self-interest.* San Francisco: Berrett-Koehler.

Bryson, J. M., & Crosby, B. C. (1992). *Leadership for the common good.* San Francisco: Jossey-Bass.

Clinton, H. (1996). *It takes a village: And other lessons children teach us.* New York: Simon & Schuster.

Haas, H. G. (with Tamarkin, B.). (1992). *The leader within: An empowering path of self-discovery.* New York: HarperCollins.

Higher Education Research Institute. (1996). *A Social Change Model of Leadership Development* (3rd ed.). Los Angeles: Author.

Knobloch, L. (Ed.) (1996). *Leadership for the new millennium: Application guidebook for the social change model of leadership.* DePere, WI: St. Norbert College.

Putnam, R. D. (1995). *Bowling alone: America's declining social capital. Current, 373,* 3–10.

Wingspread Group on Higher Education. (1993). *An American imperative: Higher expectations for higher education.* Racine, WI: The Johnson Foundation.

Chapter 5

New Ways of Leading in a Networked World

Cynthia Cherrey and Kathleen Allen

Would the CEO of the Internet please stand up? Could we even identify a single person with the knowledge and power necessary to order a sudden or drastic change in what is quickly developing into one of the most powerful communication tools? There is no such person to be found. The Internet, governed loosely by a broad range of persons, is a harbinger of institutions to come—sophisticated networks of people and resources that cannot be "managed" using current models of leadership. Leading in this networked world will require new approaches to leadership development on our college campuses.

This chapter will:

- describe the impact of living in a networked world;
- discuss why networks require a shift to non-hierarchical leadership; and
- identify new ways of leading that move beyond hierarchical leadership.

Our world of work is shifting from fragmentation to connectivity. This shift is fueled by the increased use of technology and mass communication in our lives, as well as the growing global economy. The following describes the characteristics of a fragmented hierarchical world and the corresponding characteristics of a networked world.

FROM A HIERARCHICAL WORLD TO A NETWORKED WORLD

Characteristics of a Fragmented/Hierarchical World

Under a fragmented, hierarchical approach, the whole system is understood as a collection of parts, much like a car that is constructed on an assembly line.

Each of the individual parts of a car is linked together in specific ways to insure that a driver can control the speed and direction of the final result. The car (or the whole system) can be broken down to its parts and reassembled endlessly. If the ignition switch fails, the defective part is replaced and the car can perform exactly as it did before. A good mechanic can diagnose the specific problem easily and repair the car with a new part that functions the same as the old one. The assumption behind the design of a car is that the whole is the sum of its parts.

Traditional hierarchies are examples of this fragmented worldview. Most hierarchical organizations create departments or divisions (parts) that have responsibility for specific functions (like a fuel pump or ignition switch). The CEO, like the driver of a car, is expected to be able to control the speed and direction of the organization. The organization (like the car) has distinct boundaries from its outside environment (like the road in relation to the car), and yet it is designed to have effective access to resources in the environment, as well as contribute to it.

A fragmented approach can be identified by certain characteristics. The first characteristic is how an organization is viewed as a collection of parts. The working assumption is that failure results from a defective part that, once replaced, will allow an organization to function again.

Second, hierarchical organizations have boundaries that are distinct from the external environment as well as distinct divisions within these organizations. Higher education, for example, illustrates both of these divisions. The ivory tower image of the academy represents a self-contained entity, secluded from the outside environment. Within higher education, academic and student affairs are divided by traditional boundaries between parts.

Third, fragmented hierarchical organizations tend to change incrementally. Since they are more stable and predictable they have a tendency to change more slowly. Change is viewed as being manageable and directed from the top down in the organization. Higher education organizations have a reputation for not changing their organizational structures.

Positional leaders of a fragmented hierarchy assume that the whole organization can be controlled from a key point in the system. Like the driver in a car, the CEO is the individual who is perceived as being able to control the speed and direction of the organization. Many of the assumptions about change in higher education flow from this point; the phrase "change has to start at the top" is an example of the nature of change in hierarchical organizations.

The reality described above is familiar to those of us working within higher education. Many examples demonstrate to us that we live in hierarchies operated from a fragmented orientation. We have engaged in incremental change and asserted and defended our boundaries. We have been asked to control individual employees' and students' behaviors, as well as organizational productivity. However, the dawning of a networked world does not supplant, but encompasses, a hierarchical fragmented orientation by adding another layer of dynamics to the organizations within which we operate.

Characteristics of Networks

A networked world operates differently from one built on hierarchies and fragmentation. The Internet, for example, illustrates some of the paradoxes of network dynamics and new methods of maintaining order. The Internet has a basic structure within which individuals and organizations can operate and create. The structure of the Internet consists of nodes and links. Each node is a center in a web of connections, and in turn, each of these nodes has web-like connections with other nodes. This structure is simple yet allows for great flexibility and evolution in web design and content. Within this basic structure, the opportunities for individual initiative and creation are endless. In fact, the locus of intelligence in a network shifts to the active participants of the system (Negroponte, 1995). Like the Internet, non-hierarchical leadership requires individuals who are willing to be actively engaged, rather than passive followers, to make decisions. It allows collaborators rather than boundary builders to flourish. To be successful in a networked world, we must develop new capacities and encourage the development of these capacities in students.

Networked organizations have characteristics different from fragmented hierarchical organizations. Networks do not replace hierarchical structures, but over time they change the nature of hierarchical processes and functions. While networks all have hierarchical aspects (for example, search engines on the Internet provide another level of order to web pages), they bring a significant amount of linkage that traditional hierarchies lack. Fragmented, parts-oriented hierarchies that protect their internal and external boundaries do not facilitate such linkages. However, a networked world erodes these boundaries to create a connected reality to our work that transcends the characteristics of traditional fragmented hierarchical organizations.

Networked organizations have evolved since the Industrial Revolution and as society has moved into the knowledge era. They have been called non-hierarchical organizations and post-industrial organizations. For the purpose of this chapter, network is used because it best describes the changing nature of our society, which can be identified by the following characteristics.

First, networks are thick webs of intersecting connections and cannot be understood by being broken down into individual connections. They demand to be seen as whole systems, visible only from a distance of time or space. For example, we must remove ourselves from the dance party and go to the balcony to get a true sense of the dance floor. The dynamics of the web of activity also require such distance.

Second, due to their high degree of connectivity, networks create blurred boundaries in organizations. A variety of links spans traditional boundaries, making it impossible to maintain the type of distinct boundaries that exist. If one connection is taken from the web, the flow of information uses alternate routes to its destination. In recent years, the traditional boundaries of higher education have eroded. Community service, increased internship opportunities, and parental involvement, as well as political, social, and economic issues have penetrated the academy. These changes challenge us to reconsider the type and quality of traditional curricular and co-curricular programs.

Third, networks are always experiencing dynamic change. When many highly connected variables are in play, high speeds and a great deal of movement become natural characteristics of the system. We experience this movement in the way problems seem to mutate, the increase in the number of novel problems that appear each year, and the diminishment of the rules that used to give us a sense of predictability. A corollary to dynamic change is an accelerating sense of speed. In fact, we have all gone through a collapse of time with the onset of e-mail, voice mail, fax machines, and networked computer systems on our campuses. The expectations that our staff, faculty, and students have for immediate response have increased radically. Where there used to be "float time" (much like the three days it took for a check to clear the bank) between the request for service or information and response, now there is none (Hock, 1996).

Fourth, networks can be influenced, but they cannot be controlled. A networked system is always affected by variables that exist outside the organization. This makes it impossible to know everything or understand all the intervening variables when we make decisions. Due to the dynamic movement and high degree of connectivity, networks do not respond to force; in fact, networks resist force. For example, wet sand, if we step in it, performs similarly to a network. Wet sand resists the imprint of a foot slapped down on it; however, when a foot is placed in the sand slowly, the wet sand allows the foot to sink into it. This capacity to make an imprint by "placing and waiting" is like the influencing strategies we use in groups. When we are called upon to influence the culture in a residence hall or the leadership in a student organization, we know from experience that influencing works better than force. The same is true of networks. The more people we have who are intentionally nudging a networked system in the same direction, the more we can influence the direction of the network.

The characteristics of networks have become increasingly familiar to all of us in higher education. Over the last decade, we have felt the increased rapidity of change and the lessening effectiveness of control strategies. We have encountered more people who have opinions about how we do our jobs and blurred boundaries between our divisions and the outside community. Global, economic, political, and societal issues affect our campus, our students, and the dynamics on campus. Formerly, effectiveness was measured in part by an individual's ability to maintain autonomy and protect personal boundaries. Now, effectiveness is dependent on a person's ability to develop and maintain relationships that cross boundaries and see the whole system, not just his or her part. New rules have replaced old rules. The old rule that states "Everything will become

Table 5.1
Characteristics of Fragmented and Networked Orientations

Fragmented/Hierarchical	Networked Orientation
Parts perspective	Whole-system perspective
Distinct boundaries	Blurred boundaries
Change incrementally	Dynamic change
Can be controlled	Can be influenced

clear when I grow up," has been replaced by the need for constant learning and letting go of old ways of doing things.

We often find ourselves caught between old practices and evolving standards of effectiveness because the differences between how fragmented hierarchies and how connected networks work have not been articulated. A summary of the characteristics of fragmented hierarchies and connected networks is listed in Table 5.1.

Over time, all of us have been adjusting to the incorporation of connected networks into our traditional hierarchies. This spiral of connectivity feeds dynamic movement, which feeds complexity, which in turn feeds the need for learning, which is necessary for organizations to evolve continually and thrive within the turbulent environment.

IMPLICATIONS FOR LEADERSHIP DEVELOPMENT

Clearly, our leadership development programs are currently ill-prepared to develop students who will be expected to operate within a networked world. As the world becomes more and more connected, we will be challenged to develop student leaders who can contribute effectively to this world. This goal will be difficult to achieve unless we are willing to transform ourselves and our organizations in a way that facilitates the connections and the learning we need to accomplish our own transformation.

What role can our student leadership programs play in this transformation? How can we prepare our students for leading in a networked world? In our higher education leadership programs, we must develop new strategies based on an understanding of a networked world. These strategies must flow from understanding the systemic dynamics of organizations.

As stated earlier, a networked world operates on linkages and connections. To increase the effectiveness of leading in a networked world, we need to teach means of facilitating these connections in our leadership programs. This implies reframing the underlying assumptions on which our leadership development programs are based to assumptions that embrace a non-hierarchical leadership framework for a networked world.

Underlying Leadership Assumptions

One's position and location in a hierarchical organization often predetermine one's underlying assumptions for the appropriate means of relating in that organization. Additionally, autonomy is highly valued, which results in a controlled orientation toward relationships. In a networked world the underlying assumptions that support new ways of relating include:

- Never underestimate the interrelatedness that exists within a system. The traditional view minimizes the number of connections that demand our attention. Underestimating interrelatedness becomes a liability as networks and connections increase.
- Variables in a system mutually shape each other. The traditional assumption is that there are a few independent variables that can predict many dependent variables. In a networked world, the number of variables in play increases radically due to the openness of the system. When these variables interact they mutually shape one another.
- Networks change differently than do traditional hierarchies. Networks are highly dynamic, and therefore, change is constant. Because networks are open systems, the number of variables in play also increases, and in turn, increases the level of complexity.
- In a networked world the underlying assumptions that support new ways of influencing change are:

  —Multiple persons intentionally influencing in the same direction are needed to create change. The traditional view of change is that one person initiates it and often the person at the top of the organization is given credit. However, in a network collaboration is necessary for influencing change.

  —Change can be triggered from anywhere. Traditional assumptions suggest that change can be initiated only from key positions within an organization and must be backed by organizational resources. In networks, change can be initiated from anywhere because the resources that can be used to influence the system are available to everyone in the network. The resources needed to influence change in a networked system are relationships, ideas, and shared commitment to a common intent.

In a networked world, learning is constant. Continuous learning is the means by which organizations adapt to changing conditions in the external environment. On an individual level, learning integrates knowledge with capacities and practice. On an organizational level, shared learning takes the integrated learning of many individuals into a collective organizational intelligence. In a networked world, the underlying assumptions that support learning are:

- Learning is social—it occurs in concert with others. Traditionally our school systems have structured learning as an individual activity. In a networked world, individual learning will be, by nature, limiting. Therefore learning with others and sharing differences facilitates a more holistic understanding of the nature of the networked world.

• We can never learn enough or unlearn enough—therefore continual learning and unlearning is critical.

Traditional hierarchical leadership assumptions suggest that leaders are individuals who hold positions of authority. In the constantly changing networked world, individuals in positions of authority do not have as much power because networks do not have a single lever to pull to start the assembly line of change. Nor do positional leaders have enough information to understand fully the whole system. Leadership in a networked organization can be understood only through a systemic set of actions, not the actions of a lone individual. Therefore, in a networked world:

• Leadership facilitates the process. Traditional leadership assumptions focus on vision and the direction of leadership and may suggest that the means justify the ends. Due to the connectivity of a network, the way we do things becomes as important as what we do. For example, in our leadership development programs it is important to pay attention to how we communicate with others, how we involve others, how we build community, if not more so than the task to be accomplished.
• There are many agents of leadership dispersed throughout a networked organization. Leadership within a networked world can be practiced from anywhere. In this sense, leadership has the potential of being abundant especially if we think of it as nonpositional—not just attached to position and rank. If leadership capacities are encouraged and developed, anyone in the network can become an agent of leadership.

This new way of thinking involves learning how different variables relate to and affect each other. We have the opportunity in our leadership development programs to teach ways to see the whole instead of the parts and ways to understand how variables will affect each other over time. It also involves teaching new capacities for students to be effective in a networked world. The following are suggested capacities to incorporate into leadership development programs.

CAPACITIES FOR NON-HIERARCHICAL LEADERSHIP DEVELOPMENT

Non-hierarchical leadership requires us to redesign the leadership competencies in our leadership development programs. These leadership capacities have an organizational and individual application.

Collaboration. On an individual level the capacity of collaboration requires the development of trusting and trustworthy relationships formed in the context of authenticity. If we have relationships built on trust we will be more open and able to collaborate with others. In addition, if we are authentic with others, we bring into our relationships the capability to disagree with respect. Authenticity is necessary for individual relationships and is also a prerequisite for collaboration on an organizational level. On an organizational level this capacity involves cultivating collaborative relationships. Collaboration is absolutely necessary to the change process in a networked system.

Continual Learning. On an individual level this capacity involves becoming an integrated learner. Integrated learners continue to create feedback loops between the domains of knowledge, developing new skills, and their daily practice in order to accelerate and inform their learning and insights. Individual integrated learning is necessary to facilitate shared learning on an organizational level. Facilitating shared learning is the organizational leadership capacity needed for continual learning. Due to constant change, groups and organizations need to accelerate the amount of shared knowledge, insights, and learning they acquire so they can adapt and thrive.

Diversify Perspectives. Appreciating different perspectives, a requirement for understanding a networked system, has to start with our individual responses to diversity. Questions such as: "Do our students value and respect difference?" "Do our students believe that diversity enhances and enriches their personal lives?" are important to have in mind when designing our leadership development programs for students. In addition, we need to ask these questions of ourselves maybe even before we ask them of students. Leveraging multiple perspectives is the organizational leadership capacity needed for diversifying perspectives. A network has a diverse number of viewpoints, all of which are necessary to understand the whole. As individuals thrive on diversity, organizational learning requires different perceptions to more fully understand a network.

Profound Change. Profound change is the capacity that contributes to new ways of influencing change on both personal and organizational levels. Personal transformation is the individual capacity needed for the facilitation of organizational change. Most individuals will not change if the opinion leaders of an organization are not willing to do themselves what they are asking of others. The college experience is often a time of personal transformation for students. Assisting them through their personal development and helping them to understand that the transformation of an organization influences and shapes their own transformation is a part of the learning that could occur in our leadership programs.

Systems Cognition. Seeing connections within a system or network is the individual capacity of systems cognition. Networks thrive on connections. Students become "systems thinkers" when they see how their group fits with the entire institution and when they see how their past behavior affects the present and the future. Once students can see systems, they can apply this knowledge to leveraging the dynamics of the organization and then actively influence change.

CONCLUSION

This chapter described a new way of leading, which in turn facilitates developing shared learning, influencing change, and relating ideas and people in ways that cross boundaries. When we shift our paradigm from fragmented, hierarchical, and industrial thinking to a networked mindset, we can discern simpler and more effective ways of accomplishing our goals.

We have a responsibility to reframe our leadership development programs to respond to the challenges of a networked world. Our students will influence the world in greater proportion than their numbers. Higher education needs to fulfill its promise to these students and society by preparing students to live and work in a networked world. Our students learn, in part, by watching what we do as individuals and institutions. If we are to prepare students for the twenty-first century, we must work to transform our leadership programs and our institutions. The time is now.

REFERENCES

Hock, D. (1996, October 1–3). *Systems thinking*. Keynote address at the Systems Thinking Conference, San Francisco.
Negroponte, N. (1995). *Being digital*. New York: Knopf.

Chapter 6

Using Postmodern Feminism to Reconceptualize "Citizenship" and "Community"

Lori E. Varlotta

INTRODUCTION

The same bipartite goal that drives American higher education frames the non-hierarchical leadership programs that are burgeoning on campuses throughout the country. Succinctly stated, that goal is to strengthen the democratic community by helping students develop their identity as citizens who strive for the common good. Though seldom acknowledged in any explicit way, this preeminent goal of higher education in general and leadership programs in particular rests primarily upon two political philosophies—liberalism[1] and communitarianism.[2] Both philosophies exist as the deep-seated cornerstones of leadership programs. That is, they respectively inform, albeit mostly in covert ways, leadership educators' understanding of citizenship and community. In an effort to unearth leadership's entrenched foundations, this chapter initiates the type of theoretical conversation that should—but often does not—accompany the concrete leadership programs that many of us plan and implement on our own campuses. The conversation is an important one for several reasons.

First, leadership programs can serve as powerful mechanisms for connecting theory to practice. But unless leadership's foundational philosophies are unveiled, how can students directly link them to the practices those theories are meant to inform? Shouldn't students be able to name and describe the type of citizenship their leadership programs promote? Similarly, shouldn't they, as leaders, be equipped to analyze the type of communities they are building and maintaining?

Second, leadership educators and their students should determine whether the philosophies that currently configure "citizenship" and the "democratic community" should continue to do so. If leadership paradigms are shifting as quickly and dramatically as many contemporary scholars suggest (Higher Education Research Institute [HERI], 1996; Komives, Lucas, & McMahon, 1998), shouldn't the foundations upon which these paradigms rest shift as well?

Third, if the foundations are shifting, leadership educators should be guiding these changes. Leadership educators must help their students determine, for example, the type(s) of philosophy that best describe(s) the citizen of today and the citizen of tomorrow. In addition, leadership educators should help their students identify the type of philosophy that accurately conceptualizes the complex communities built and maintained by contemporary citizens.

Divided into three sections, this chapter addresses these very issues and questions. Section one summarizes liberalism and communitarianism so that educators can better understand these important philosophies and the ways they covertly inform current configurations of citizenship and community. Section two reviews how these philosophies—in a combined form that I call a "theoretical amalgam"—shape the work of Benjamin Barber, one of leadership education's key theorists. Concerned that Barber's theoretical amalgam limits and simplifies the ways educators and students think about and practice leadership, section three introduces postmodern feminism. This final section uses postmodern feminism to reconfigure citizenship and the democratic community in ways that may ultimately strengthen the other process-based models of leadership discussed in this volume (i.e., The Social Change Model of Leadership and the relational model developed by Komives et al., 1998).

LEADERSHIP'S TRADITIONAL "ME/WE" DICHOTOMY: THE LIBERAL CITIZEN/THE COMMUNITARIAN COMMUNITY

Almost every time I talk with students who are participating in the *SKILL Initiative*, a campus-wide, non-hierarchical leadership program at the University of San Francisco, the conversation focuses on the development of citizens and the promotion of the democratic community. Despite the complexity of each of these terms, I am usually surprised by the ease in which students define them.

When I ask students to brainstorm the meanings that we, members of the American academy, attribute to the term "citizen," a flood of responses fills the room. Within minutes, their "citizen is/citizens are" list looks something like this:

- An individual member of a state, country, or territory. In our country, this membership entitles us to life, liberty, and the pursuit of happiness.
- Someone who participates actively in the communities to which he/she belongs.
- Individuals who, at least in terms of the law, are equal to each other.
- Political players who continually balance "rights" with "responsibilities."
- Community members who can work the system to get things accomplished.

The Liberal Citizen

If you did the same brainstorming exercise on your campus, I suspect the definitions of citizenship generated by your students would mirror those presented by mine. Whether students know it or not, "citizenship" is now, and has long been, defined by a political philosophy called "liberalism." Though it is more complex than this, liberalism can be described briefly as a philosophy that theorizes the primacy of the individual citizen (for the purposes of this chapter, "the ME") over the democratic community ("the WE"). Because the individual citizen occupies the privileged position within liberalism, liberal philosophers have spent considerable time and energy defining the term. For liberals, "citizen" refers to the rational, autonomous, equal members of the state who enjoy the freedoms associated with democracy.

Interestingly, the liberalism that underlies today's collegiate leadership programs is the same philosophy our founders invoked as they drafted our inchoate nation's defining documents: the Constitution of the United Sates of America, The Declaration of Independence, and The Federalist Papers. As the longevity of these documents reveals, the liberal rhetoric that frames them is not only an ingrained part of American history, but of present-day life as well. But should contemporary leadership educators continue to allow the basic tenets of liberalism—rationality, autonomy, equality, freedom—to double as the defining features of contemporary citizenship? To examine that important question, let us review those tenets.

Rationality. Liberals define rationality as the capacity for reasoned mental activity. Moreover, they consider rationality to be at the very core of an individual's identity. Rationality is the common essence that all individuals share. It is the very capacity which differentiates men and women from other living species—that which defines them as "human."

Equality. When liberal philosophers talk about citizens, they are likely to describe them as being equal to each other. But their use of "equality" refers to a potential capacity rather than to an actual state of being. In liberal theory, then, men and women share the *potential* for equality despite the concrete inequalities that mark the material world.

Autonomy. Liberals believe that the essence of humanness (i.e., rationality) and other human characteristics (autonomy, freedom, and equality) are properties of autonomous individuals rather than "connected" individuals or social groups. Accordingly, an individual's identity (as a citizen or otherwise) is autonomous and exists independently of social context. In this view, autonomy is defined as "self definition [and] a reliance on the authority of individual judgment" (Jaggar, 1988, p. 44).

Freedom. When liberals talk about "freedom" they are frequently referring to one of two types: (1) "freedom from the state," a type of laissez-faire institution with minimal constraints; or (2) "freedom to" rule themselves as equal members of the democratic state.

As these tenets reveal, liberalism is grounded upon a "me versus we" foundation. "The ME," the individual citizen clearly takes priority over "the WE," the democratic community. Objecting to such privileging, other philosophers, called communitarians, have formulated a political theory that privileges community as a response to and criticism of liberalism.

The Communitarian Community

By revolving their philosophy around the notion of community, communitarians reverse the "ME/WE" dichotomy with one best described as "WE/ME." For communitarians, "community" denotes a consensual entity grounded in and bound by a "common good." Interestingly, this is the same understanding of community that most students hold. While presenting leadership workshops throughout the country, I have asked students to define community. Their collective "a community is" list looks something like this:

- A group of people who live or work in close proximity to each other.
- A group of people who share similar ideas, politics, values, convictions, and/or religious beliefs.
- A unified group that cares about each other and the things they have in common.
- A communal state of being and a warm-and-fuzzy feeling.
- A group who works together to reach common goals and pursue similar dreams.
- A feeling of belonging and a sense of togetherness.
- The unity amidst diversity.

Though most students would not label it as such, their notion of community has been shaped directly by a communitarian philosophy. Moreover, it is the philosophy that underlies the Social Change Model of Leadership. Thus, it makes sense to review here the communitarian notion of community.

First, the communitarian community is an entity that reflects common values, common norms, and shared goals. As such, members of a community must work to reconcile competing and conflicting demands, expectations, and responsibilities. In this view, communities value commonality and uniformity.

Second, most communitarians reject universal norms, purposes, and goals by arguing that individual communities define what is good and right for their particular members. Thus, the meaning of "rights" and "goods" must be connected to a particular social context; without such a context, their meanings are empty.

Third, communitarians typically theorize the type of community that individuals are born into (e.g., national communities, state communities, "tribes," families). Basic communitarianism, then, focuses primarily on the communities to which individuals are *necessarily* connected rather than those to which they *choose* to belong (e.g., neighborhood groups, special interest clubs).[3]

Finally, communitarians believe that individuals are constituted by the relationships they share with others. Accordingly, they posit the community, or the "WE," rather than the individual, or the "ME," as the most fundamental human phenomena. From their perspective, communities exist prior to individuals. Human significance and purpose are derived by and through the community. Unlike liberals who see the individual as extracted from his/her social contexts, communitarians assert that individuals derive both their existence and their identity from the relationships they share with others.

Though brief, this review of liberalism and communitarianism exposes an important point. Leadership's foundational philosophies both rest upon a bifurcated foundation that separates the individual from the community. As illuminated above, liberals maintain the "ME/WE" dichotomy. Communitarians sustain the dichotomy but simply reverse the privileged position by favoring the "WE" over the "ME."

LEADERSHIP'S EMERGING AMALGAM

Recognizing the tendency that some educators have to sketch educational communities as a series of oppositions, or dichotomies, Benjamin Barber, political scientist and Director of the Walt Whitman Center for Democracy at Rutgers University, asks educators to conceptualize "both/and" rather than "either/or" configurations of community. As explicated below, his own notion of community is informed directly by both liberalism and communitarianism.

Review of Barber's Strong Democratic Community

Known for his many writings and presentations on leadership and politics, Benjamin Barber is one of the most cited theorists in leadership education.[4] Typically, leadership educators use Barber's work to reinforce the type of democratic community they strive to create and maintain on their own campuses. Indeed, Barber's "strong democratic community," theorized in detail in his 1984 book, *Strong Democracy*, has become the ideal endorsed by many leadership theorists and practitioners (Astin, 1996; Couto, 1994; Giroux & McLaren, 1984; Morse, 1990; Newmann, 1990). In conceptualizing the strong democratic community, Barber evokes both liberalism and communitarianism. This means his community is neither configured solely in the liberal vein as a collection of autonomous, self-interested individuals nor in the communitarian one as a consolidated hegemony that erases individuality, autonomy, and equality. Instead, the "strong democratic community" is the place where rational, autonomous agents are transformed into *citizens* "through participation in common seeing and common work" (Barber 1984, p. 232). Importantly, citizens must identify with others, *as citizens*; otherwise, "unhealthy and antidemocratic" (Barber 1992, p. 245) associations form and flourish: "If we cannot bond as citizens [in the name of democracy] we will probably bond . . . as gangs, secret societies, conspiratorial political groups, and hierarchical clubs . . . in the name of race or ethnic origin or gender, accentuating adversarial differences in . . . insidious ways" (Barber 1992, p. 245).

According to this passage, democratic communities derive their very existence from the salubrious forms of communal association maintained by citizens who strive for the common good. For Barber, the common good is actualized when citizens focus on the similarities rather than their differences. Thus, he urges citizens to try to put themselves in the place of others and to "strain to hear what makes [them] alike" (1984, p. 175). *Conformity* and *similarity* are two of the characteristics that mark the democratic community, but Barber suggests that they are *whole* and *bounded* as well: "[C]ommunities function only when their members conceive of themselves as empowered to participate fully in the common activities that define [that] community. . . . [Communities] rooted in freedom do not come in fragments and pieces. You get it all, or you get nothing" (1992, p. 228).

Barber's strong democratic community (1984) begins with equal citizens who see, hear, and want similar things. The community is strengthened as these citizens work towards the common good. And the community culminates, as a bounded whole, when "consensus arising out of undominated discourse to which all have equal access" (Barber 1992, pp. 213–214) has been reached.

Analyses of Barber's Community

On the surface, Barber's conceptualization of community as one that combines liberal notions of "equality," "freedom," "autonomy," and "rights" with communitarian ones of "citizenship," "common good," and "communal affiliation" looks good. After all, it places both the liberal "me" and the communitarian "we" in equally important positions. In a sense, it can be understood as a ME ⇔ WE model that dissolves the dichotomy that artificially separates and ultimately privileges the individual *or* the community. Given the bipartite goal of most collegiate leadership programs, Barber's theoretical hybrid is better suited to inform these programs than either of the single philosophies from which it is derived. But before leadership educators endorse Barber's theory as "the best" one, let us probe a little deeper.

To a large extent, Barber's theory of the strong democratic community is an "additive" one because it simply combines the liberal "ME" with the communitarian "WE." Rather than scrutinize carefully the constitutive parts of each philosophy, Barber leaves them intact. His notion of the "liberal citizen," for example, is based on the assumption that individuals are born free and equal. Furthermore, he conflates "citizenship" with the legal status individuals hold against the state. Unfortunately, this conflation maintains the artificial dichotomy between public and private—a dichotomy that "regulates to the private all particularity and difference" (Mouffe, 1992, p. 377), thereby acting as a powerful, albeit covert, mechanism of exclusion. Meanwhile, Barber's "communitarian insistence on a substantive notion of the common good and shared moral values is incompatible with the pluralism that is constitutive with modern democracy" [and collegiate leadership programs] (Mouffe, 1992, p. 378). By fashioning the individual citizen in the liberal mode and the strong democratic community in the communitarian mode, Barber ultimately, though inadvertently, *limits* the ways leadership educators think about, talk about, teach, and practice non-hierarchical leadership.

To reconceptualize citizenship and community, then, in ways that reinforce rather than ignore the pluralism of the academy, leadership educators must invoke a different type of philosophy. I have found postmodernism in general, and the writings of Chantal Mouffe and Shane Phelan in particular, to be well-suited for this task. Because postmodern feminism, in particular, has been created and sustained by those who attempt to highlight difference, make sense of conflict, and foster healthy types of tension, it offers great potential for transforming the ways educators and students think about, talk about, and do leadership.

Using Postmodern Feminism to First Deconstruct and then Reconstruct the Concepts and Practices of Leadership Education

"Postmodern feminism"[5] is a highly complex and polylithic discourse. For the purposes of this chapter, it might be generally understood as both a "deconstructive" and "reconstructive" philosophy. In terms of the former, postmodern feminism deconstructs the "communitarian community" and the "liberal citizen" discussed above. It terms of the latter, it reconstructs "community" and "citizenship" in a different mold to reflect more accurately the realities at play in collegiate leadership programs.

Postmodern feminists resist leadership educators' tendencies to fashion citizenship from the liberal "ME" and community from the communitarian "WE." Rather than accept any complete or coherent notion of "we" or "me," they argue that these terms connote the multiplicities embedded in any "single" group or any "sole" individual. Their deconstruction shows how any "me" is constituted by an "I" and a "you" and how any "we" by an "us" and a "them." Writings by Chantal Mouffe (1992) and Shane Phelan (1995) explicate this point.

Consensus and the Common Good

As summarized above, Barber's strong democratic community rests upon an all-inclusive "we." This whole, bounded, and coherent group ("the WE") utilizes consensus as it strives in unison for the common good. According to Mouffe, this conceptualization of community is seriously flawed because the construction of any "we" necessarily creates a "them." Mouffe insists, therefore, that both the democratic community and the process that fuels it, (i.e., consensus) are necessarily grounded in *exclusion* rather than *inclusion*: "The definition of a 'we' always takes place in a context of diversity and conflict. . . . [O]nce it is accepted that there cannot be a 'we' without a 'them' and that all forms of consensus are, by necessity, acts of exclusion, the question cannot be any more the creation of a fully inclusive community" (Mouffe 1992, p. 379). As exclusivity can never be fully avoided, Mouffe's intent is not to escape it but to expose how it operates covertly in most communities.

When leadership educators ignore or gloss over exclusivity, they suggest falsely that the views of those who reach consensus accurately reflect the views of everyone. When leadership educators conflate the consensual "we" with "everyone" and "our views" with "their views," they encourage (consciously or unconsciously) student leaders to talk about, speak for, and act on behalf of others (e.g., "followers," "collaborators," "constituents," and so on). For educators who wish to contest this pedagogical practice and the discourse that informs it, Mouffe offers some interesting insights. In "Feminism, Citizenship, and Radical Democratic Politics" (1992), Mouffe challenges theorists and practitioners alike to see how and why consensus and the common good function as "vanishing points: something to which we must constantly refer when acting as citizens, but that can never be reached" (1992, p. 379). By theorizing consensus and the common good as the vanishing points of community rather than the respective process and outcome of community, Mouffe recognizes explicitly (1992) citizens' allegiance to the democratic principles of equality and liberty and the multiple and competing interpretations to which these principles lend themselves. For educators to tease apart the complexities embedded in the democratic discourse, the principles it shapes, and the practices it prescribes, they must probe the complexities of their own identity as "citizens." The work of Phelan and Mouffe can be used as this very probe.

Citizenship

According to Phelan, every "we" and each "I" embody partial, but multiple, overlapping and conflicting identities (1995). This notion of identity creates "citizens of the lack" (Phelan, 1995, p. 337). "Lack," as it is used here, means that no individual is completely contained by one category; and no category neatly encompasses an entire group of individuals. Phelan, therefore, rejects the liberal notion that an individual is constituted by a coherent identity and the communitarian notion that a bounded community reflects the common good of all of its members. If leadership educators support Phelan's argument, they should teach students to be cognizant of and willing to act upon their affinities and sympathies—reminding students all along that their sympathies and affinities "need *not* be total to be real and effective" (Phelan, 1995, p. 251 [emphasis added]).

To a large extent, Mouffe's conceptualization of citizenship parallels Phelan's "citizens of the lack." Like Phelan, Mouffe resists the liberal notion that citizenship emerges through a person's coherent and fixed identity. Moreover, Mouffe rejects another key assumption endorsed by liberals: She does not believe that all citizens are necessarily equal to each other. The category itself (i.e., "citizen"), Mouffe insists, has been created by a patriarchal system to reflect a particular type of masculine image. Unless it is reconfigured, the concept of "citizen" negatively affects those who do not fit this mold (Mouffe, 1992). To reconfigure "citizenship" in a way that averts such an impact, Mouffe supplants the democratic assumption of equality with the following postmodern assumptions:

"Citizen," like all other forms of identity, must be conceived as socially constructed, multifaceted, and fluid. For Mouffe, citizens renegotiate their individual identity by being mindful of the multidimensionality (e.g., the "Is" and the "yous") that establishes it. For Mouffe, there is no coherent "ME" that constitutes citizenship. Each person's identity, as citizen and otherwise, is formed by the multiple "selves" a single person embodies throughout his/her lifetime. Citizens renegotiate both their individual and collective identity constantly by focusing on the affinities they share temporarily with other similarly complex individuals. A female citizen, for instance, is of course, "a woman." Still, her identity (as a citizen) is not shaped simply by her "womanhood." After all, her citizenship is formed also by her race, socioeconomic class, societal status, religion, occupation, and so forth. The multidimensionality of an individual's identity helps explain the heterogeneity of all groups. Thus, it may make rhetorical sense to talk about "women," "men," "blacks," "whites," and so on. But, none of these groups is homogenous: These groups neither connect all their respective individuals (all women, all men, all blacks, all whites) to each other nor to the correlative practices, actions, and allegiances superficially associated with these groups. In other words, it is neither the case that all women are the same nor that all female citizens will uniformly support "women's" issues. Likewise, it makes little sense to assume that all men are exactly alike or that all male citizens will completely support "men's" issues.

Citizens are united, albeit temporarily, not by the process of consensus described in the first half of this chapter but through a process called "articulation" (Mouffe, 1992). Unlike consensus, articulation does not identify or produce a common good that uniformly reflects the stable interests of those who reached consensus or those the consensual decision-makers represent. However, articulation does establish nodal points—the nonpermanent loci created by citizens who share a particular, albeit temporary, interest. In this view, a "Black History Month" nodal point, for example, may be constructed by students who are interested in promoting the understanding, appreciation, and visibility of Black history. It is the *interests* of these students—not their *identity* (as defined by race, ethnicity, or anything else for that matter)—that prompts them to temporarily fix a "Black history" nodal point. In other words, this particular nodal point will attract African-American students, other students of color, and white students who share an interest in issues related to Black history.

As demonstrated above, Mouffe and Phelan retain the terms commonly deployed by leadership educators. By relying on postmodern feminism, however, they redefine them in interesting ways: the common good is a vanishing point (Mouffe, 1992); consensus is a social imaginary (Mouffe, 1992); and citizenship is a nonessential and fluid identity (Mouffe, 1992; Phelan, 1995). Their deconstruction of each of these terms changes their meanings significantly. And these changes mark the first step in reconstructing a different version of "community."

Reconstructing a Different Type of Community

In reconceptualizing community, Linda Singer (1991), another postmodern feminist, utilizes different descriptors to mark the definitive features of what she coins the "community at loose ends." Unlike Barber's strong democratic community, one that is bounded and whole and marked by consensus and conformity, Singer's community neither refers to a "collective will" nor to a shared sense of being. Rather than understand "community" as a pre-given entity maintained by those who share a common origin or nature, Singer describes community as that which is continuously created and recreated by the forces of need and desire *and* the forces of resistance, denial, and conflict. The "elasticity" of this community is its appeal, "an appeal that operates not as a presence but as a discourse, exchange, and difference" (Singer, 1991, p. 125).

Rejecting consensus, equal citizenship, and the common good—the definitive features of the democratic community—Singer uses elasticity, discourse, and difference to set her "community at loose ends" apart from the one that circulates as the norm in most collegiate leadership programs. For the following reasons, Singer's conceptualization of community has the potential to broaden the ways educators think about, talk about, teach, and practice leadership.

First, because the "community at loose ends" is constituted by members who embody multiple, conflicting, and overlapping identities, no one person is expected to be the spokesperson for any group, and no single group is perceived to be the "owner" of any cause/issue. This important point liberates and challenges students in meaningful ways. It should not be presumed, for example, that a Cinco de Mayo program should be planned solely by and for Latino/a students. Furthermore, as there is no single or pure Latino/a identity, no Latino/a student should be expected to represent "the" Latino/a perspective. While Latino/a students are sure to be involved in the program, the planning and implementation should also include any other student who is interested in exploring the significance of Cinco de Mayo. Once planned, the program should target multiple audiences: those who have much to learn and those who already know quite a bit about the issues at hand.

Second, just as the identities of individual members are fluid and multiple, the identity of the overall community is fluid as well. A "community at loose ends," therefore, must be resilient enough to reflect a diverse and changing membership. After all, in any leadership program, student participants come and go, advisors change, people rotate in and out. Students must learn, therefore, how to negotiate and renegotiate the identity of the group—elastic though its membership may be.

Third, a "community at loose ends" is at least partially created and maintained through discourse. Some of this discourse should probe the constitutive terms that define community. It is precisely because there is broad, albeit superficial agreement (in most collegiate leadership programs) regarding the meanings of democracy, consensus, citizenship, and the common good that terms like these are undertheorized and unproblematized. But as revealed above, none of these terms are neutral or benign. When left unquestioned, these very terms tend to normalize (and hide) the exclusivity and subordination upon which they rest. To avoid this tendency, leadership educators must ask questions that unveil what these terms presume, preclude, and propose: "Whose" good is reflected in the "common" good? Whose voices are amplified during "consensual" decision-making processes? And whose voices are muted in that same process?

CONCLUSION

If leadership educators use postmodern feminism (rather than a liberal-communitarian amalgam) to inform their non-hierarchical leadership programs, the following positive shifts may occur:

From the "Consensual Community" to the "Critical Community." Postmodern feminism will prompt leadership educators to change dramatically the ways they talk about community. When leadership educators talk about "community," they currently rely on what I call the "Cs of consensus" (Varlotta, under review). That is, they talk primarily about the common good, common purpose, conformity, and commonality. Granted, these terms (especially in the reconfigured forms present here) partially describe the communities created and maintained by leadership programs. But to reflect those communities in more accurate ways, educators should invoke also the "Cs of criticality": conflict, confrontation, contestation, contention, challenge, change, constructive criticism, continual creation, and compromise. In other words, leadership educators must consciously supplement the "Cs of consensus" with the "Cs of criticality" any time they describe "community."

From Consensus to Compromise. In non-hierarchical leadership programs, students are more likely to reach an informed compromise than a complete consensus. In working toward informed compromise, students must be able to explicitly acknowledge the various values, beliefs, and traditions that were contributed *and* forfeited during the process. Accordingly, students must see whose values, beliefs, and traditions were maintained (and why) and whose were expelled (and why). Teaching students to compromise does not foreclose the possibility of temporary and partial consensus, but it does reveal how consensus is often formed by and through the exclusion of certain voices.

From Comfortable to Conflicted. Because postmodern-feminist-informed leadership programs bring tensions, challenges, and confrontations to light, it is not unusual for students to leave a leadership program feeling conflicted rather than comfortable. When this occurs, educators must remember and students must learn that ambiguity, agitation, and uncertainty often serve as powerful impetuses for further exploration.

From Identity Politics to Interest-Based Action. Postmodern feminists' criticism of unitary and essentializing identities (both at the individual and community level) does not mean that they abandon identity categories or unified politics. But it does mean that political activities should never be reduced to some fictitiously uniform group. To be productive and positive, political action should revolve around common interests, intentions, and struggles. Importantly, the basis of this commonality must be in chosen points of "social possibility," not in *a priori* points (over which we have little control) and not in shared experience of oppression and victimization. Scholar, political activitist, prolific writer, bell hooks says it well:

Many people mistake a critique of the universalizing ethos with the rejection of commonalty and common bonds. They collapse the two. I feel that it's not that we want to do away with the notion of commonalty, but that we want to find the basis of commonality in something other than a notion of shared experience or common oppression. . . . [Educators must encourage students] to think about solidarity rooted in chosen points of bonding and contact. You know, we do not choose our ethnicity, we do not choose the neighborhoods we grow up in . . . we must learn to think in terms of common [chosen] points. (hooks, 1996, pp. 231–232)

Leadership educators do not commonly evoke postmodern feminism to inform their own conceptualizations of citizenship and community. But for reasons elucidated throughout this chapter, such an alliance might prove beneficial. By unearthing some of the problematic assumptions that covertly ground the current conceptualizations of these terms, postmodern feminists deconstruct the theories and practices that unquestionably circulate as norms in leadership education. Deconstruction is not the only work fueled by postmodern feminists, however. As revealed above, the work of these scholars facilitates "construction," too. Hence, if leadership educators want to fuel social change by constructing a community that recognizes, appreciates, and fosters difference, multiplicity, and discourse, then they might want to extract leadership from the democratic discourse in which it is currently embedded and resituate it within a postmodern feminist one.

NOTES

1. "Liberalism" does not exist as a static monolithic philosophy. When used throughout this chapter, however, the term is used to reflect those themes—equality, justice, autonomy, and fairness—that loosely connect "modern liberalism" and "classical liberalism." Two popular forms of classical liberalism may be attributed to Locke and Rousseau. Roughly speaking, Lockean liberalism viewed liberty as freedom *from* the state. In this view, the state should be a laissez-faire one with minimal constraints. Rousseauean liberalism, on the other hand, held that liberty is the freedom *to* rule oneself as a member of an equal democratic state. In his view, the enlargement of the state's power is justified if it works to liberate people from oppression. There are (at least) two forms of modern liberalism—the libertarian liberalism of Robert Nozick and the social contract theory of John Rawls—loosely (and respectively) rooted in the aforementioned strands of classical liberalism. Robert Nozick (1974) rejects John Rawls' welfare-state-liberalism (1971) by resisting the Rawlsian claims that inequalities are permissible when they benefit the least privileged members of society. According to Nozick (1974), Rawls has strayed from classical liberalism's concept of the minimal state by espousing his redistributive "justice as fairness" theory. Rawls's seminal book, *The Theory of Justice*, deploys the hypothetical "original position" to depict how rational individuals might enact their sense of justice in ways that would create a just society. For detailed accounts of these theories of liberalism, see J. Rawls, *The Theory of Justice* (Cambridge, MA: Harvard University Press, 1971); and R. Nozick, *Anarchy, State, and Utopia* (Oxford: Blackwell, 1974).

2. "Communitarianism," to some extent, is understood as a response to liberalism. Accordingly, it questions the primacy of liberalism's autonomy, equality, and justice by framing its central position around notions of the common good, social responsibility, and interdependence. Rather than work primarily for "freedom from" or "freedom of the state," as might liberals, communitarians work for the revitalization of a community that is bound by the common good. For a more detailed account of communitarian philosophies, see M. Daly, *Communitarianism: A New Public Ethics* (Belmont, CA: Wadworth Publishing Company, 1994).

3. Resisting the prototypical communitarian community, dubbed "community of place," Marilyn Friedman (1992) theorizes "communities of choice." See her article, "Feminism and Modern Friendship," in S. Avineri & A. de-Shalit (Eds.), *Communitarianism and Individualism* (Oxford: Oxford University Press, 1992).

4. Barber has authored 10 books. Those referenced frequently by leadership educators include *Strong Democracy* (1984); *An Aristocracy for Everyone* (1992); *The Conquest of Politics* (1988); *The Artist and Political Vision*, edited with McGraph (1982); *Liberating Feminism* (1975); and *The Death of Communal Liberty* (1974). In addition to these texts, Barber is a prolific writer of political essays. His essays regularly appear in *Atlantic Magazine*, *Harper's*, the *New York Times*, the *New Republic*, and many other magazines and scholarly journals. PBS's *Frontline* is producing a television special based on some of his work. Others may hear about his work at one of the lectures he delivers to universities, educational associations, and advisory boards throughout the country.

5. In some sense "postmodern feminism" may be thought of as a multifaceted set of reactions to certain types of philosophies (e.g., modernism, liberal feminism, cultural feminism, etc.) and the assumptions associated with these philosophies (e.g., objective

knowledge, the coherent self, essentialized groups, etc.). The term is used throughout this chapter *not* to reflect a diametrical opposition to the aforementioned philosophies (or any others, for that matter). Generally speaking, the term is used here to interrogate the covert power and privilege embedded in the democratic discourse that typically frames collegiate leadership programs. The label itself—"postmodern feminism"—is used specifically to refer to those theorists who explicate how power and difference play into the construction of individuals' identities, the relationships they form, and the communities they build.

REFERENCES

Astin, A. (1996, March–April). The role of service in higher education. *About Campus*, 14–19.

Barber, B. (1984). *Strong democracy*. Berkeley: University of California Press.

Barber, B. (1992). *An aristocracy of everyone*. New York: Oxford University Press.

Carnegie Foundation for the Advancement of Learning. (1985). *Newman report of higher education*. Princeton, NJ: Author.

Couto, R. (1994, September 1–4). *Teaching democracy through experiential education: Bringing the community into the classroom*. Paper presented at the annual meeting of the American Political Science Association, New York.

Daly, M. (1994). *Communitarianism: A new public ethics*. Belmont, CA: Wadsworth Publishing Company.

Friedman, M. (1992). Feminism and modern friendship: Dislocating the community. In S. Avineri & A. de-Shalit (Eds.), *Communitarianism and individualism* (pp. 101–119). Oxford: Oxford University Press.

Giroux, H., & McLaren, P. (1986). Teacher education and the politics of engagement: The case for democratic schooling. *Harvard Educational Review, 56*(3), 213–238.

Haraway, D. (1990). A manifesto for cyborgs. In L. Nicholson (Ed.), *Feminism/Postmodernism*. New York and London: Routledge.

Higher Education Research Institute. (1996). *A Social Change Model of Leadership Development* (3rd ed.). Los Angeles: Author.

hooks, b., & Trend, D. (1996). Representation and democracy: An interview. In D. Trend (Ed.), *Radical democracy: Identity, citizenship and the state* (pp. 228–236). New York: Routledge.

Jaggar, A. M. (1988). *Feminist politics and human nature*. Totowa, NJ: Rowman & Littlefield.

Komives, S., Lucas, N., & McMahon, T. (1998). *Exploring leadership: For college students who want to make a difference*. San Francisco: Jossey-Bass.

MacIntyre, A. (1984). *After virtue: A study in moral theory* (2nd ed.). Notre Dame, IN: Notre Dame University Press.

MacIntyre, A. (1988). *Whose justice? Which rationality?* Notre Dame, IN: Notre Dame University Press.

Morse, S. (1990). Developing a capacity for civic judgment. In J. Kendall et al. (Eds.), *Combining service and learning: A resource book for community and public service* (Vol. I, pp. 225–233). Raleigh, NC: National Society for Internships and Experiential Learning.

Mouffe, C. (1992). Feminism, citizenship, and radical democratic politics. In. J. Butler & J. Scott (Eds.), *Feminists theorize the political* (pp. 369–384). New York: Routledge.

Newmann, F. (1990). Reflective citizen participation. In J. Kendall et al. (Eds.), *Combining service and learning: A resource book for community and public service* (Vol. I, pp. 76–86). Raleigh, NC: National Society for Internships and Experiential Learning.

Nozick, R. (1974). *Anarchy, state, and utopia.* Oxford: Blackwell.

Phelan, S. (1995). The space of justice: Lesbians and democratic politics. In L. Nicholson & S. Seidman (Eds.), *Social postmodernism: Beyond identity politics* (pp. 332–356). New York: Cambridge University Press.

Rawls, J. (1971). *A theory of justice.* Cambridge, MA: Harvard University Press.

Rawls, J. (1994). Justice as fairness. In M. Daly (Ed.), *Communitarianism: A new public ethics* (pp. 71–78). Belmont, CA: Wadsworth Publishing Company.

Sandel, M. (1982). *Liberalism and the limits of justice.* Cambridge: Cambridge University Press.

Singer, L. (1991). Recalling a community at loose ends. In Miami Theory Collective (Eds.), *Community at loose ends* (pp. 121–130). Minneapolis: University of Minnesota Press.

Young, I. (1997). Asymmetrical reciprocity: On moral respect, wonder and enlarged thought. *Constellations, 3*(3), 340–363.

Section II

Putting Theory into Action: Successful Campus Programs

REFLECTIONS FROM UCLA STUDENTS

Even the most complex bureaucracy can assume the characteristics of nonhierarchical leadership simply by welcoming the independent expression by all personnel within an organization. The point when every position in a group or company is perceived as equally important and necessary to an adequately functioning whole is the point when an organization assumes non-hierarchical values.

—Joe Manko

I did not join the Bruin Leaders Project because of my overwhelming desire to improve my leadership skills. As a matter of fact, I thought my leadership training had become complete. As far as I was concerned, I embodied everything a leader was and should be. That sounds very arrogant, but that was not my attitude. Instead, leadership was this abstract concept that had been tossed around all through high school, and as long as I wasn't passive or idle, I was considered a leader. Likewise, leadership seemed to be something you were born with or not. Honing your leadership skills seemed like taking voice lessons to become a rock star: you could only do so much and go so far unless you had the innate predilections. Therefore, when I was nominated to be a member of the Bruin Leaders Project, I viewed the nomination as an invitation to shape other students' training in leadership, not extend my own. However, just the opposite occurred. The organization began to take a spiritual slant for me. I could go to class to cultivate my mind, go to the gym to beautify my body, but UCLA seemed to lack venues in which I was encouraged to look introspectively at my soul and my direction. Where was I going? I knew my major. I knew what I wanted to do. But there is so much more to life than a career.

—Sarah J. Hansen

Chapter 7

Developing an Interdisciplinary Doctoral Program in Leadership Studies

Mark T. Green, Jacquelyn Alexander, and Ray Boryczka

OVERVIEW

Traditionally, graduate programs focus on a single academic discipline such as education or business. This time-honored method produces graduates who possess extensive knowledge in a specific academic discipline but limited knowledge in related disciplines. Additionally, this tradition perpetuates the often narrowly defined expertise of the faculty teaching in the discipline as they engage primarily with colleagues and students from the same academic discipline. This chapter discusses the emerging need for interdisciplinary degree programs, the idea of teaching leadership as an interdisciplinary program, and lessons learned in the creation of an interdisciplinary Ph.D. Program in Leadership Studies at Our Lady of the Lake University (OLLU), a private, Catholic university in San Antonio, Texas. The curriculum developed addresses many aspects of leadership, including non-hierarchical leadership themes. Additionally, throughout the collaborative development, change management, and implementation phases of the program, non-hierarchical leadership principles were employed.

Forces Driving Interdisciplinary Degree Programs

Graduates of academic programs typically apply their knowledge in organizational settings such as schools, corporations, or government agencies. Almost all organizations of the next millennium will become increasingly more complex and require new skills of their members (Ensign, 1998; Bartlett, 1989). Because of factors such as advanced technology, the move of society to a more multicultural view of leadership, and the rise in a global economy and workforce, OLLU is updating its approach to many of its graduate programs.

Technology. The 1990s explosion of powerful technologies that enable humans to acquire information anywhere at anytime is literally the tip of an iceberg. Inexpensive access to powerful technology is transforming organizations into environments in which internationalism, virtual products, and workers will become the norm. By 2005, microchip speeds will be roughly ten times faster than those of today, yet cost 50 percent less (Gates, 1999). As a result of continually increasing microprocessor speeds and decreasing costs, organizations of the twenty-first century will be able to inexpensively and easily communicate globally. International, desktop video conferencing will become as commonplace and inexpensive as a local phone call today. Collaboration with real-time data among international work teams will become as simple as e-mail has become in the 1990s. In the eighteenth century, Adam Smith's *Wealth of Nations* (Smith, 1776/1994) described a workplace in which labor was divided and workers performed repetitive, specialized tasks with mechanistic precision. In the twentieth century, the rise in knowledge workers and the service industry have prompted authors such as Margaret Wheatley (1999) to describe organizations using a biological paradigm. Rather than a rigid, machinelike view of the workplace, Wheatley describes the modern workplace as an adaptive, self-organizing organism. Leading workers in mechanistic workplaces requires different skill sets than leading workers in organismic workplaces.

Multiculturalism. Technological developments will drive organizations to become not just multicultural within a city, state, or country, but truly, globally multicultural. As a result, organizational leaders will need different leadership skills from those of a less diverse and technologically advanced time.

The Wisdom of Interdisciplinary Teams. Many organizations have reacted to increased complexity caused by technology and more diverse workplaces by using team-based problem solving. The argument traditionally advanced for the use of teams is that teams bring a wider range of experiences and perspectives to complex problems. Because of the even more radical technological changes ahead, graduate programs that prepare students for team-based work must begin to prepare students to perform well in diverse interdisciplinary teams. (Nahavandi & Aranda, 1994)

Teaching Leadership as an Academic Interdiscipline. Principles and theories of leadership are often incorporated piecemeal into many college and university programs. For example, business schools teach leadership as a derivative of management and business. History and political science departments analyze great leaders, organizational dynamics, and political tactics. Schools of education teach leadership specific to schools. The list of academic programs that incorporate leadership themes in traditional coursework is long.

OLLU's interdisciplinary doctoral program draws on concepts and theories from the leadership literature and from leadership principles taught in traditional disciplines. By extracting leadership ideas from many academic disciplines, the interdisciplinary Ph.D. program is able to provide a more concentrated and rich academic experience in the emerging discipline of leadership studies than if it were to take a traditional, discipline-bound approach.

Leadership Studies Versus Leadership Training. Many leadership training institutes and academies with a primary focus on the interpersonal behavioral traits of effective leaders already exist. While such training may be beneficial to the recipients, this behavioral approach is limited. First, leadership training tends to overemphasize the *one best method approach.* Often a highly successful leader attempts to canonize her or his method into several easily followed steps. Much organizational theory from the late twentieth century emphasizes a concept called *contingency theory.* (Saunders, 1998; Fiedler, 1972) Simply stated, contingency theory reminds us that different organizational cultures and problems require different leadership styles and interventions. The *one best method approach* to leadership training tends to work well in one specific type of culture and within a narrowly defined set of leadership challenges.

In addition to a *one best method approach*, leadership training tends to emphasize changes in interpersonal behavior. Graduates of leadership training institutes tend to increase their personal mastery and self-awareness, improve their interpersonal communication skills, and learn to *influence people.* These skills are unquestionably valuable to individuals aspiring to become successful leaders. As leaders accept roles in more complex or larger organizations, however, personal charisma and interpersonal communication skills by themselves are insufficient.

Leaders of large, complex organizations typically must add a range of historical, analytical, financial, political, and research abilities to the honed interpersonal skills required to lead small organizations. Interpersonal communication skills are necessary, but no longer sufficient when stakeholders become groups rather than single individuals.

LEADERSHIP STUDIES AT OUR LADY OF THE LAKE UNIVERSITY

OLLU developed an interdisciplinary doctoral program in Leadership Studies to move already graduate-trained professionals through a model of leadership development. During the program, students study four thematic areas: leadership, management, collaborative societal systems, and research. *Within* these themes, the first-year curriculum stresses introspection into why students hold their attitudes about work, organizations, and leadership. While the curriculum addresses traditional leadership models, emerging models such as nonhierarchical, relational, and organic models are also introduced.

During the second year, students continue to take courses across the four thematic areas, but the issues become *interorganizational.* Whereas the first year of the doctoral program focuses on systems internal to an organization, the second year helps students think in terms of an external community of systems— whether the community is social, economic, or political.

During the third year, through coursework, internships, and dissertation research, students build on their interpersonal, intraorganizational, and interorganizational knowledge to analyze and synthesize unique leadership challenges within a single sector such as business, education, healthcare, a state, or a nation.

Change—Creating an Interdisciplinary Ph.D. in Leadership Studies

Founders of OLLU's Interdisciplinary Ph.D. in Leadership Studies developed a cogent vision in response to the many changes that they believed lay ahead for graduate education and organizations. Regardless of the soundness of a vision, however, institutions tend to resist change. In his seminal book *Leading Change*, John Kotter (1996) outlined eight major steps to follow when presenting change issues to an organization. The first four steps focus on developing the change; the last four steps focus on consolidating the change into the organizational culture. In introducing the interdisciplinary Ph.D., members of the founding group followed the first four of Kotter's steps. Members are still working through steps five through eight in the second year of the doctoral program.

Steps in the Doctoral Program Proposal

Kotter's Step 1—Establish a Sense of Urgency. To inaugurate change, Kotter recommends organizations first establish a sense of urgency. Important aspects of creating urgency are to set targets high, use consultants for external perspectives, and bombard members of the organization about changes that are inevitable. To establish momentum for a proposed Ph.D. in leadership, the founders hired an educational consultant from a leading institution with recent experience with similar programs. The consultant provided data on changes in graduate education and customer needs to create the case for change and a sense that the time was right for an interdisciplinary Ph.D. at OLLU.

Kotter's Step 2—Form a Powerful Coalition. An admired and dynamic change management team is crucial to any change effort. In the case of the interdisciplinary Ph.D., key faculty members and administrators from all academic units were invited to serve on a developmental steering committee. These members held high institutional reputations for wisdom and fairness. Two faculty members from the School of Business, a faculty member from the College of Arts and Sciences who had previously served as Vice-President and Academic Dean, and two faculty members from the School of Education and Clinical Studies (SECS) comprised the developmental steering committee. The Dean of the School of Education and Clinical Studies chaired the committee and the Vice-President and Academic Dean served in an *ex officio* role. The steering committee provided a safety check, which consisted of *admired fair-agents* who held high institutional reputations for placing the greater needs of the university before specific departmental wishes. When the committee recommended the de-

Chapter 10

The Peer-to-Peer Context

Sunshine B. Martin

Technological advances and a new world order have demonstrated the need for new concepts of leadership that promote a shared sense of "global community." This chapter will outline the strategic planning process utilized at the University of Nevada, Las Vegas to create a comprehensive leadership development program to help prepare our students to assume leadership roles in today's society. The program uses the Social Change Model of Leadership Development (SCM) (Higher Education Research Institute [HERI], 1996) as a foundation and involves students in all aspects, including program design, implementation, and evaluation.

STRATEGIC PLANNING PROCESS

The University of Nevada, Las Vegas (UNLV) is a public, four-year, urban institution with over 22,000 students. Ninety-five percent of students commute from Clark County, home to the city of Las Vegas, and 25% are non-traditional in age.

In 1995, UNLV welcomed a new President to campus who engaged the university community in a process of dialogue and planning intended to establish clearly the future of the institution. Through this strategic planning process a working document was created, outlining seven university goals. Three of the university goals relate to student leadership: to become more student focused, to create an inclusive and just campus community, and to communicate and collaborate more effectively (University Planning Committee, 1996).

With the emergence of a collective vision for the university came the need to assess current practices and devise new ways to meet the needs of students at UNLV. In conjunction with the planning process, the Division of Student

Services formed a Leadership Process Group to act as a vehicle through which the division could address the need for leadership development interdepartmentally. The goal of the Leadership Process Group was not only to create an approach to "leadership," but also to develop strategies through which the division could collaboratively recruit, educate, and develop student leaders. Through a review of the literature, the Leadership Process Group adopted a working definition of leadership, "the process of making intentional choices to foster a more ideal state for self and others" (Bennis and Goldsmith, 1994; Burns, 1995; HERI, 1996; Kuh, Schroeder et al., 1994). This definition was presented to staff and students through informal focus groups to reveal their thoughts and ideas regarding leadership.

The Leadership Process Group discovered a distinct qualitative difference between the general student perspective and that of professional staff. Students seemed to view leadership as a set of skills or qualities, that is, "who you are as a person," while staff generally regarded leadership as goal accomplishment, or "what you do as a person." Both students and staff questioned agreed that altruistic behavior is at the heart of leadership, a perspective that is reinforced by the literature encouraging new models of leadership development that are value or quality based, rather than skill or goal driven.

Seeking a leadership development model that incorporated the perspectives of both students and staff, the Leadership Process Group submitted a recommendation to utilize the SCM as a foundation for all leadership development initiatives. The SCM was chosen in part because it reflected the perspectives of both staff and students in that it is supportive of the notions of altruism, personal integrity, and action. The use of the SCM allowed for a common definition of leadership, a common language, and a framework to create multiple leadership development programs that are complementary and build on students' previous experience. (See Bonous-Hammarth [Chapter 4 in this volume] for a broader discussion of the SCM.)

In the spring of 1996, the Leadership Process Group drafted a document outlining their findings and recommendations. This document was presented to the professional staff in the Division of Student Services and the major student governing bodies (Student Government, Residence Hall Association, the Greek Councils, and the Ethnic Student Council). The recommendation to utilize the values set forth in the SCM as criteria in the development and design of new projects as well as a lens through which to review current programs was adopted unanimously by students and staff. The working definition of leadership became, "the process of identifying a need and working collaboratively with others to affect positive change."

PEER-TO-PEER EDUCATION

The adoption of a non-hierarchical leadership approach on a university campus required a philosophical shift that transcended organizational structure.

UNLV, like most institutions of higher education, has a bureaucratic or hierarchical structure. Likewise, most student groups, modeling the university or United States government, have divided responsibilities into identifiable positions and have implemented by-laws and operating procedures that encourage majority rule as a means for making decisions. Translating the values of the SCM into action required that staff and students unlearn previous notions of positions and power and learn new ways of working collaboratively that cross organizational barriers.

The Leadership Process Group decided that the best way to design and implement a comprehensive leadership development program that incorporates the SCM would be to use the concepts of the Model as the standard of operation. That is, students should work in conjunction with staff toward a common purpose of providing non-hierarchical leadership development opportunities. Peer-to-peer interaction is one of the principle developmental influences on college students (Astin, 1993; Pascarella & Terenzini, 1991). Many leadership programs, such as ropes or challenge courses, have successfully utilized peer-to-peer discussions combined with experiential learning activities (Rastall, 1996). Taking this concept to the next level, UNLV created a program that not only involves peer-to-peer discussions but also includes students in the planning process and incorporates students as peer facilitators.

UNLV LEAD TEAM

The decision to adopt the SCM and the conviction that peer education would be a powerful vehicle to expose students to the Model lead to the creation of the Leadership Education And Development (LEAD) Team. The UNLV LEAD Team was charged with the mission of establishing a comprehensive leadership development program with the SCM as its foundation. In the spring of 1997, the Division of Student Services opened the selection process for students to apply to part of the LEAD Team.

Students with extensive leadership experience at UNLV and with diverse campus affiliations were targeted to ensure new leadership initiatives were inclusive of programs already in existence. Professionals from Student Activities, Greek Life, and Campus Housing agreed to co-advise the LEAD Team with consultation from the Office of Multicultural Student Affairs. The contributions of students and staff advisors of varying affiliations assisted the LEAD Team in bridging existing barriers between groups on campus, helping to create a comprehensive and cohesive leadership development program. For example, both Greek Life and Campus Housing already had leadership development programs in operation; these groups would be unlikely to "buy-into" a new leadership development approach unless given the opportunity to provide input on the new leadership development initiative.

Implementing the values of the SCM is more easily said than done. Initially, the five students and three staff advisors on the LEAD Team spent more time discussing how to work together than on deciding what to accomplish. Following the SCM, members of the LEAD Team first explored individual values. Through exercises and discussions, members of the LEAD Team clarified their own values pertaining to leadership development and wrote a personal creed committing themselves to the joint efforts of the LEAD Team. The next step was to learn to work together as a team and to agree to a common purpose or vision for the LEAD Team.

Using the SCM as a basis for a common language, the LEAD Team negotiated a standard of operation and group expectations. When negotiating roles, the LEAD Team agreed that students and staff would have equal input into the decision-making process, but that the students on the LEAD Team would have primary responsibility for program implementation, with the guidance and assistance of the staff advisors.

After three months of exploring group values, learning to work together as a team, and assessing the needs of the campus community, the LEAD Team adopted a vision statement:

We will increase the group's expertise and build a framework for the future by increasing membership.

We will be a cohesive group of recognizable, friendly, and knowledgeable individuals with proven leadership qualities—we will share our expertise with others and challenge each other.

We will encourage a university-wide effort to blend the lines between organizations and governing bodies to create seamless leadership and collaboration among university departments and student organizations.

We will increase the effectiveness of established and emerging leaders through the creation of a comprehensive leadership development program.

The Social Change Model will be utilized as a foundation for the creation of all programs; we will offer opportunities to explore individual, organizational, and community awareness. The exploration of leadership values will be complemented by the skill development needed to actualize the Model.

We will become a model of positive change through which we will be recognized as a leadership development organization on the UNLV campus and gain national recognition to share our ideas and knowledge with others.

THE LEADING EDGE SERIES

Since professional staff at UNLV had agreed to incorporate the Model into leadership-training initiatives for current student leaders, the LEAD Team focused initial programming efforts on emerging student leaders. In the fall of 1997, the LEAD Team offered the first LEADing Edge Series, a ten-week leadership series designed to expose students to the SCM. The series lasted for two hours per week, was co-curricular, and was publicized primarily to first year students through New Student Orientation, Campus Housing, and newsletters to first year commuter students.

The students on the LEAD Team were responsible for all aspects of the LEADing Edge Series including publicizing, planning, designing interactive sessions, facilitating discussions, and serving as mentors for students enrolled in the series. Prior to each session the student facilitators agreed on the experiential activities that would be utilized and selected a facilitator to have primary responsibility for each exercise. Likewise, the facilitators also decided on appropriate discussion questions. Each facilitator served as a mentor to a small group of the participants. The small groups allowed participants to share their opinions and experiences to a depth not practical during the large-group discussions.

Week one served as an introduction to the series. Participants were introduced to each other through icebreakers and participated in an exercise that introduced the SCM. Additionally, participants were divided randomly into small groups and were given an opportunity to share their expectations for the series with the student facilitators. During the first week, participants were asked to complete a pre-assessment instrument and were informed that a recognition banquet would be held during week ten for all participants who completed the series successfully. Successful completion entailed attending at least seven of the first nine weeks.

At the heart of the LEADing Edge Series were the Seven Cs of the SCM: consciousness of self, congruency, commitment, collaboration, common purpose, controversy with civility, and citizenship. Each week participants were asked to build on their prior experiences by exploring a different C through interactive exercises and small and large group discussions. For example, during the week focusing on congruency, the facilitators held a mock auction. Participants were given a set amount of play money and were provided the opportunity to bid on a list of values. The limited amount of money forced the participants to prioritize their values and literally "put their money where their mouths were." The small group discussions not only focused on which values participants "bought" and why, but also on the concept of "walking the talk." Students shared personal experiences often about instances when their actions were not congruent with their values.

The advisors attended each session and sometimes interjected comments during the large-group discussions; however, the facilitation and small-group discussions were the responsibility of the student facilitators. After each session the advisors and facilitators met to review the evaluations from the participants and to give each other feedback. Between the weekly sessions, the student facilitators contacted each of the participants by telephone to maintain communication and help the participants to feel connected to the program.

Week nine of the series was designed to bring the Seven Cs together. After spending a week examining each C, students engaged in dialogues about how the SCM can be actualized. During these discussions the focus was on UNLV and how students might use the SCM to effect positive change within the campus community. Based on these conversations, some of the students have formed new groups to address issues on campus. For example, one group felt that students were uninformed about events and programs held on campus and so it worked with the student newspaper to include a section on upcoming campus events. Another group of students worked with faculty and staff to create the first ever UNLV Cultural Leadership Retreat to address a perceived need on campus.

The LEAD Team developed a much-appreciated recognition program. Students who completed the series successfully received a personalized invitation to the closing banquet. Also invited by the LEAD Team to the semiformal event were faculty and administrators who were supportive of the program and students who had completed the series in the past. The banquet has become a reunion for students who share the common experience of participating in the LEADing Edge Series. At the banquet, current "graduates" have an opportunity to offer a short testimony of their experience in the series and what they plan to take with them.

Evaluations from the LEADing Edge Series have been overwhelmingly positive. In particular, students rate highly the peer facilitators, the interactive exercises, and the use of the SCM. On assessments conducted one to two semesters after completion of the LEADing Edge Series, students report the series contributed to increases in self-confidence and understanding of their own values. A large majority of the participants have assumed leadership positions within other campus organizations since attending the series. These students report that the series is very useful in their endeavors to work with others toward a common purpose. Perhaps the most significant impact of the series is revealed in students' changing definitions of leadership. The pre- and post-assessments reveal a distinct movement from viewing leadership as a position to viewing leadership as a process. Students' definitions of leadership often include the concepts of collective action and common good after completing the LEADing Edge Series.

EXPANSION OF THE LEAD TEAM

While pleased with the first semester implementation of the LEADing Edge Series, the LEAD Team recognized that many of the original goals of the group had not yet been attained. Lack of time seemed to be the biggest barrier, so the LEAD Team opted to expand and create subcommittees, each of which would be responsible for accomplishing a different objective. Returning LEAD Team members divided into three committees, and new members were selected so that each committee had four to six students. One committee, the LEADing Edge Facilitators, continued to coordinate all aspects of the LEADing Edge Series. The two new committees, the Involvement Coordinators and the Organization Consultants, focused energy on new projects.

The Involvement Coordinators were students dedicated to helping other students to become involved on campus. This committee was formed in response to feedback received during the LEADing Edge Series: Many students indicated that they signed up for the series because they wanted to get involved but did not know how. The SCM emphasizes that anyone can be a leader, so the Involvement Coordinators' goal was to empower students to take action within the UNLV community. The Involvement Coordinators compiled a list of involvement opportunities published in the Student Handbook/Planner, designed a video presentation for New Student Orientation, did classroom presentations, and published a monthly newsletter.

The Organization Consultants, the third LEAD Team committee, developed three priorities: (1) to assess and process the needs of student organizations; (2) to provide resources that promote organizational growth; and (3) to establish, develop, and maintain partnerships with student organizations. As an introduction to the campus, the Organization Consultants hosted a Student Organization Officer Training Retreat. The training followed the concepts of the SCM, providing student officers with resources and leadership skills needed to actualize the Model. The Organization Consultants used this retreat as an avenue to build relationships with officers and to encourage student organizations to form collaborative partnerships.

To gain further information regarding the leadership development needs of the various student organizations, the Organization Consultants developed an assessment tool for organization officers, members, and advisors. Based on the results, the Organization Consultants created a leadership resource library, offered "brown-bag" leadership trainings for officers and advisors, and created the *Student Organization Handbook*.

The efforts of the LEAD Team are supported by professional staff advisors who use the SCM in discussions and leadership trainings for student groups. The Division of Student Services sponsors a one-day student leadership conference each year. This conference, called Leadershop, uses the SCM as a foundation. It is coordinated by a committee of students and staff. To support students' efforts to actualize the Model further, UNLV opened the Student Organization Resource Center (SORCE). The SCM encourages students to take collective action and make a positive impact, so it is important to have a structure in place that augments their efforts. SORCE provides student organizations with workspace, computer access, photocopying services, message and mail services, poster-making and office supplies, and access to campus policies and resources. The LEAD Team office and the Leadership Library are also located in SORCE.

Systems have been created to reinforce new attitudes and behaviors that reflect a non-hierarchical approach to leadership. For example, the Division of Student Services revised the Student Leadership Scholarship application and selection criteria to reinforce the LEAD Team's definition of leadership. Instead of asking students to submit lists of leadership positions they have held, the Division of Student Services asks students to document situations in which they had identified a need and worked collaboratively with others to effect positive change.

ROLE OF THE ADVISORS

The LEAD Team is a student group that operates within the values of the SCM. While most advisors are accustomed to taking a non-authoritative approach to working with student groups, the LEAD Team is unique because of its non-hierarchical structure. Other than the division into three working committees, the LEAD Team does not identify positions of authority; there is not a president, secretary, or even a chair. All members have an equal level of responsibility.

Using the SCM as a framework, the LEAD Team agreed to a set of standards and expectations. Throughout the year, especially when difficulties arise, the LEAD Team returns to these shared standards. Since the LEAD Team does not operate with the traditional division of duties, it seems that a significant amount of time is spent negotiating roles. For example, all members agreed at the LEAD Team retreat that each committee would meet weekly and that all three committees would meet together every other week. Each committee has six students and one primary advisor, allowing the committee meeting format to be open discussion. When members agree to an action plan, each person volunteers to take responsibility for his or her part. However, when the entire LEAD Team meets every other week, there are suddenly eighteen students and three advisors in one room. Currently the responsibility of creating an agenda and managing the meeting rotates from person to person; however, this is not a perfect system. Sometimes the meetings feel unpredictable or unproductive because each student has a different style of running the meetings; the lack of consistency allows for certain items to fall through the cracks. The LEAD Team has recently decided to establish an administrative sub-committee to be responsible for meeting management and the selection process. Learning to work together, especially within a non-hierarchical structure, is a continuing process.

One of the challenges for the advisors of the LEAD Team is helping members negotiate roles without intervening in the group's process. Students learn more about themselves and non-hierarchical leadership when the advisors take a non-directive role; that is, when the advisor ensures by words and actions their lack of authority in situations where the group needs to have consensus (Dunkel & Schuh, 1998). Since the students on the LEAD Team are peer educators responsible for providing leadership development opportunities for other students, the advisors must find a balance between empowering the group and ensuring the needs of the general student population are met. Periodically, advisors need to challenge individuals if commitments are not honored. Due to the non-hierarchical structure of the LEAD Team, students feel comfortable providing each other with feedback as well.

IMPACT OF USING A NON-HIERARCHICAL APPROACH

Observations at UNLV indicated that peer-to-peer interaction is a strong vehicle for engaging students in discussions about non-hierarchical leadership. Students seemed more willing to discuss leadership values, and the ways in which a non-hierarchical approach to leadership was possible, with other students than with faculty or staff. In evaluations students reported that the SCM was more easily understood through experiential exercises and group discussions than through a lecture format. According to these evaluations, one of the advantages of the SCM was its flexibility and broadness; students accepted the core values readily and engaged willingly in meaningful conversations regarding the Seven Cs. Students who were exposed to the Model through numerous avenues and multiple sources were more likely to grasp the concepts and recognize the value of having a common language and a common understanding of the definition of leadership.

While implementing the SCM is a continuous process, some visible benefits of adopting a non-hierarchical approach to leadership have been immediately evident at UNLV. There has been an increase in collaboration among the various student groups. This was particularly observable through interactions in the Student Organization Resource Center and was also evident in the groups that have connected to cosponsor campus programs. Additionally, university officials have noticed that the way in which students approach issues of concern has changed. More and more, students reported that they see themselves in a partnership with the university administration. Rather than merely complaining about particular campus policies, many students attempted to work with other students and staff to make a change. For example, a student on the Task Force for an Inclusive and Just Campus Environment recently spearheaded the formation of the Public Safety Advisory Board to give students a voice regarding the policies and practices of the campus police department.

Quite often the bureaucratic or hierarchical structure of the university impeded a true non-hierarchical approach. In these instances some students struggled with the inconsistency between the values of the SCM and realities of the university's structure. For example, UNLV student government uses Roberts Rules of Order as a standard of operation during the student senate meetings. While these rules can often be an effective means to make decisions, at times some students have become distraught with the inability to discuss a topic openly. The language these students used indicated a philosophical shift from "majority rule" to "common good."

In conclusion, complete integration of a new, non-hierarchical approach to leadership at an institution takes commitment on multiple levels: administration, faculty and staff, and students. Simply exposing students to a new model is not enough. Systems need to be in place to reinforce and reward new attitudes and behaviors. It is the gradual shift in the campus climate and the increasing circle of students and staff that understand and practice the SCM that has kept the

LEAD Team excited about entering its fifth semester of existence on the UNLV campus. A non-hierarchical approach to leadership has encouraged students to be active participants in the campus community and has helped prepare students with the skills and experience needed to make a difference in today's global society.

REFERENCES

Astin, A. W. (1993). *What matters in college?* San Francisco: Jossey-Bass.

Bennis, W., & Goldsmith, J. (1994). *Learning to lead: A workbook on becoming a leader.* Reading, MA: Addison-Wesley.

Burns, J. S. (1995). *Defining leadership: Can we see the forest for the trees?* Manuscript submitted to the Journal of Leadership Studies.

Dunkel, N. W., & Schuh, J. H. (1998). *Advising student groups and organizations.* San Francisco: Jossey-Bass.

Higher Education Research Institute. (1996). *A Social Change Model of Leadership Development* (3rd ed.). Los Angeles: Author.

Kuh, G. D., & Schroeder, C. (1994). *The student learning imperative: Implications for student affairs.* Washington, DC: American College Personnel Association.

Pascarella, E. J., & Terenzini, P. T. (1991). *How college affects students: Findings and insights from twenty years of research.* San Francisco: Jossey-Bass.

Rastall, W. P. (1996). A qualitative look at a high ropes course experience. *Journal of Student Affairs, 5,* 2–9.

University Planning Committee. (1996). *University of Nevada, Las Vegas premier urban university: A public agenda for the decade 1996–2005.* Las Vegas: University of Nevada, Las Vegas.

Chapter 11

Common Cause: Different Routes

Cynthia Cherrey, Judi Biggs Garbuio,
and Rachel Isgar

It wasn't that long ago that our primary modes of communication in college work settings were telephone, mail, and the use of faxes for urgent business. Now, we are accustomed to checking e-mail, voice mail, pagers, and cell phones, in addition to using our traditional modes of communication throughout the day and evening. One of the results of the increased use of technology in our lives and the growing global economy is that college students will work in a world of increasing change, diversity, complexity, and interdependency. To develop student leaders for this ever-changing world, we must consider the shift from our traditional paradigm of the hierarchical organization in the Industrial Era to an emerging paradigm of a networked world. Hierarchical organizations driven by the industrial paradigm are characterized by a "parts mentality," an emphasis on boundaries and incremental change. In contrast, the networked world features a holistic perspective, blurred boundaries, nonlinearity, and dynamic change. (See Cherrey and Allen [Chapter 5 in this volume] for a more detailed discussion of the significance of the shift from traditional hierarchical models of organizations to a networked paradigm.)

Students often feel the university experience is fragmented or decentralized. For example, students attend classes on a regular basis, but they might see separate academic advisors to guide them through the registration process. Moreover, financial aid, housing, meal plans, and parking are all separate, distinct offices that reflect the "parts" mindset of a hierarchical organization.

The traditional college is often viewed as the "ivory tower of knowledge." However, as the world becomes more and more connected, we are challenged to live and work in this ever-changing world and to develop students who can contribute effectively to this world. As educators, we have the opportunity to blur the boundaries within our organizations and beyond, to dissolve the myth of the ivory tower, and to design leadership programs that value certain aspects of the traditional paradigm while creating new initiatives to embrace the emerging paradigm.

In response to and in support of the emergence of the networked era, the University of Southern California has developed the Extended Multidimensional Approach to Leadership Development (the USC Model). This chapter will describe the USC Model's philosophical framework and review some of the leadership initiatives that illustrate USC's continually evolving approach to leadership.

HISTORICAL AND PHILOSOPHICAL FRAMEWORK

USC, a private research university, rich with tradition and an entrepreneurial spirit, is located in an urban, diverse, multi-ethnic neighborhood. The university's relationships with this community are vital to the school's mission. In fact, USC was just named the Time/Princeton "College of the Year" for its community outreach efforts. The surrounding community continues to provide a "living learning laboratory" that reflects both the traditional and emerging paradigms.

In 1991, Student Affairs created a task force to pursue the feasibility of developing a comprehensive leadership model specifically for USC that takes advantage of its urban environment. The task force included staff, faculty, and student representatives from a wide array of academic disciplines. The task force focused on one broad question: Why is leadership important to individual students and the university? The answers to this question are embedded in the institution's philosophical framework, which includes: (1) the importance of individual student growth, (2) the importance of leadership as a continuing learning process, and (3) the importance of organizational and societal change.

Individual students grapple with identity issues in an attempt to understand who they are and define their own personal values (Chickering & Reisser, 1993; Gilligan, 1977; Perry, 1981). Student leadership experiences (both formal and informal) provide an environment for participants to understand how groups work and to interact with individuals with different values and cultures. The intent of the USC Model is that students embrace the responsibility of shaping the university community and understand how the segments of a university are interconnected. Additionally, it is important to value those individuals who are "informal" leaders in a variety of contexts. These informal leaders may not be affiliated with a particular student organization; however, they help to define and shape their environment. This process encourages participants to identify, develop, and explore their own skills, values, learning, and leadership in a supportive and challenging environment.

Leadership is a continuing learning process (Komives, Lucas, & McMahon, 1998). Leadership development on our campuses ought to include individual student learning, organizational learning, curricular and co-curricular experiences (in particular those beyond the campus walls), and society at large. Student Affairs' primary role in this process is to create the initiatives and the environment in which the development of leadership capacities can occur for each student.

As a general framework the Division of Student Affairs used an integrated approach to learning that includes theory, capacity building, and practice (Senge, 1996). The Model's theory and concepts were chosen to help students grasp the subject at an intellectual level. Capacity-building was emphasized to allow students in the program to develop leadership skills and abilities. The creators of the USC Model believed that developing the leadership capacity of the university's students could transform the university experience for all students. Likewise, they felt that students who lived and worked in an interconnected, knowledge-based world, could contribute effectively to this changing world (Matusak, 1997). Finally, opportunities for students to practice leadership were created both through the curriculum and in students' daily experiences. For the developers of the USC Model, learning was considered a process with rich layers and patterns of experiences, during which students have continued opportunities for deeper understanding and integration.

Examples of USC leadership initiatives will be described in greater detail in the following sections. The underlying perspectives and levels of interaction behind the leadership initiatives will also be explored.

THE USC EXTENDED MULTIDIMENSIONAL APPROACH
TO LEADERSHIP DEVELOPMENT

USC has developed an extended, multidimensional approach to leadership development that begins in each student's first year. The framework uses the term *extended* to promote the concept that leadership development goes beyond the collegiate experience. USC's leadership development is geared to be beneficial in many areas of a postcollege career. These areas include work, community service, and family life. A goal of the USC approach is to offer a perspective of leadership that recognizes the interdependence of individuals in formal and informal groups throughout the university and community.

Underlying Themes and Perspectives

Ethical Perspective. An ethical perspective of leadership is a primary component of the USC Model. According to Bok (1988), ethical standards and integrity "grow out of a general concern for others and a desire to respect their legitimate interests" (p. 46). The USC Leadership Model uses reflective learning, collaboration, community service and role modeling to help students achieve higher ethical standards. A main component of the model attempts to increase the individual sense of ethical and social responsibility as a part of the leadership process.

Transnational Multi-Ethnic Perspective. The USC Model's emphasis on a transnational, multi-ethnic perspective is intended to assist students in becoming competent leaders in a pluralistic society. As the twenty-first century begins, we find ourselves in a global and diverse community. According to Bloland, Stamatakos, and Rogers (1994) "Prevailing student development theory ignores notions of institutional responsibility for contributing to society, to the fostering of democracy and democratic ideals, to international understanding, or for that matter, helping students become responsible and contributing members of society" (p. 21). Leaders of the new millennium will be called upon to embrace internationalism and multiculturalism, not only in the college setting, but also in their work places and in society. The Model promotes the concept that leadership development goes beyond the collegiate experience and the value of life-long learning is instilled.

In addition, the transnational, multi-ethnic perspective of leadership is tied closely to USC's strategic plan and its goal of becoming a truly international university. Its position on the Pacific Rim makes it an important link to the Asian and Pacific island countries. USC has one of the largest international student populations of any major university in the United States (Chronicle of Higher Education Almanac, 1999).

Systemic Perspective. The leaders of the new millennium will need to have a greater understanding of our interdependent world. To be a leader who can influence change in this interconnected world, one must develop a systemic perspective. In general, a systems thinker is someone who sees the whole picture, pays attention to short-term and long-term perspectives, uses peripheral vision to see complex relationships, recognizes the complex and interdependent nature of systems, and remembers that we are all influenced by the systems in which we function (Capra, 1992; Wheatley, 1992).

New thinking on leadership calls for us to design our leadership initiatives for a broader, more holistic approach to the college experience that integrates curricular with co-curricular experiences. For example, students could use knowledge learned in a marketing class to create a proposal for a volunteer project. Whether leadership is fragmented or systemic, there are multiple levels of interaction. Leaders interact with individual students, formal or informal groups, the university community, and the global society.

Multiple Levels of Interaction

The USC leadership framework defines complexity as the interconnectedness of the individual student with various constituent groups and environments. The influence of individual students and student organizations ripples throughout the university community. In the remainder of this section, the USC framework is outlined in the four levels of interrelated interaction. USC students are encouraged to engage in these multiple levels of interaction: the individual student, the informal and formal student groups, the university community, and society.

Individual Students. The development of a student's leadership capacity is anchored in his or her self-concept, identity issues, critical thinking, and responsibilities (Komives, et al., 1998). These are all interwoven aspects of student development that are inherent in the college experience. Individuals bring to college unique backgrounds that are created by age, ethnicity, family, education, socioeconomic status, childhood experience, and work experience. These backgrounds have shaped their values and directly affect how they view leadership and society. It is important to focus on each individual's personal development and how this, in turn, affects his or her experience in higher education.

Formal or Informal Groups. Individuals can become involved with a variety of formal student organizations or informal, non-structured groups. USC offers extensive student organization involvement, from musical, theatrical, dance, and photography clubs to religious and cultural groups. An entrepreneurial spirit and diverse viewpoints are valued because they allow us to see new possibilities and innovations that may otherwise not surface. An example of a non-structured group involvement occurred when one student e-mailed a list-serve to ask about the possibility of donating the extra discretionary money on his meal plan to a homeless shelter. This simple e-mail message blossomed into a university-wide program for students to give their unused funds at the end of each semester to help the homeless in the Los Angeles area. Both formal and informal student groups are laboratories where vision, value, and purpose are explored to understand organizations and how they lead in different contexts.

The University Community. One of USC's overarching leadership goals is for the university to provide opportunities for students from all over the world, including the United States, to live together and learn from each other. As stated earlier, one of USC's strategic goals is to become a truly international university. With this in mind, USC is breaking ground for a residential college with an international theme. This residential college will incorporate personal interaction, discussions with visiting scholars, and programming initiatives and will continue to provide opportunities for students to take responsibility in shaping the university community for an even more diverse society.

Global Society. It is important to develop leaders who can be successful in an increasingly interdependent world. Interdependencies include the impact of population, environment, technology, communications, and trade issues on our future. Leadership education must be conducted in the context of a networked, global society. Thus, USC's international theme residential college will attract other internationally oriented programs and activities from campus, the community and the world.

PRACTICING LEADERSHIP AT USC

Practicing leadership and reading about current leadership concepts go hand in hand. The remainder of the chapter will focus on practical examples offered at USC for all students to illustrate further the Extended Multidimensional Approach to Leadership at USC, including: Your Portfolio, an interactive web-based learning tool; the Emerging Leader Program primarily for new students; the formation of an interdisciplinary leadership minor; and an ethnicity-based leadership program.

Your Portfolio

Technology provides students with access to information 24 hours a day, seven days a week. Your Portfolio is an on-line, interactive tool that allows students to record, reflect upon, and evaluate their education and experiences, as well as explore new avenues for involvement. Your Portfolio focuses learners on a more meaningful approach to integrating their personal and intellectual development during their tenure at USC. To articulate the university's values, Your Portfolio revolves around five themes: Enriching Your Academic Life, Understanding Yourself and Others, Planning Your Future/Career, Partnering with Your Community, and Living with Integrity and a Healthy Lifestyle. Additionally, there are four components within Your Portfolio: Strategize, Explore, Record, and Publish.

The Strategize section helps students establish learning goals to be successful at USC. For example, under the theme of Understanding Yourself and Others, students can select from the following learning goals: *begin to develop and/or refine your own philosophies and beliefs, get to know people different from yourself (i.e., background, religion, ethnicity, politics, etc.),* or *explore viewpoints different from your own.* After students have decided which learning goal they want to pursue in each of the five themes, they are sent electronically some specific tasks they can accomplish to achieve that goal. For example, if a student selected *explore viewpoints different from your own* he or she would receive: *attend programs which appear to advocate the opposite point of view from your own (e.g., political, religious, etc), attend a religious service different from your own, talk about it later with others,* and so on.

Your Portfolio is a technological map to help students navigate a plethora of programs and services. The Explore section organizes this information according to the five themes stated earlier. The users can explore student organizations, academic/research, special programs, and employment/internship opportunities. The students can then click on their choice and be linked directly to the student organization or special program of their choice.

All of the student's experiences are then documented within the Record section. The Record section integrates the three components of Senge's (1996) model: theory, capacity building, and practice. It does this by asking four probing questions: *What did I experience? What have I learned? What did I learn about myself and others? And finally, how can I make a difference with what I've learned?* The Record section allows students to use their portfolio to reflect on their progress both inside and outside the classroom and make connections between the levels of interaction: individual, informal/formal groups, university, and global. A fourth text box is designed for individual faculty members to personalize the journal entry based upon their class assignments. The fourth section, Publish, allows the students to publish an electronic resume.

Your Portfolio integrates the ethical and transnational multi-ethnic perspectives within two of the themes (e.g., Understanding Yourself and Others, and Living with Integrity and a Healthy Lifestyle). The systemic perspective utilizes technology as a tool to navigate the university as a whole. Additionally, individuals complete their respective portfolios while reflecting on their formal and informal leadership experiences while attending USC and beyond.

The Emerging Leader Program

The Emerging Leader Program (ELP) is designed to develop a group into a team of committed and able leaders, who will refine and utilize their skills during their time at USC and after graduation. The eight-week ELP program consists of two hours each week. During the first hour the students focus on leadership concepts and the second hour is devoted to capacity-building and practicing their leadership skills. An important component of the program is a community project each group develops.

The ELPers are divided into teams based upon their community service interests. The community service projects provide an experiential, reflective, interdisciplinary, and holistic focus for applying the leadership concepts to community-related issues in a practical setting. This approach also illustrates non-hierarchical leadership because none of the groups have designated, positional leaders.

The application process for ELP begins in the fall to determine participants' community service interests and ascertain why they are interested in participating in this program. The program begins in January with a retreat organized by the previous year's ELP participants. Former ELPers design, develop, implement, and facilitate the program for the entering students collectively. These students often comment on what a different experience it is for them to facilitate the discussions and organize all aspects of the program rather than be passive recipients in a predetermined program.

After the retreat, the ELP participants attend weekly leadership enhancement seminars based upon the USC Leadership Model (e.g., ethical, transnational/ multi-ethnic, and systemic perspectives). ELP incorporates the multiple levels of interaction intentionally by focusing on the participant's strengths and areas of improvement, then moving to work in small community service groups that impact both the university and surrounding community. For example, a past project with global impact featured a fundraising campaign for medical supplies for a hospital in Mexico.

ELP and Your Portfolio are fluid in nature; for example, the team of ELPers can go to the Explore portion of Your Portfolio and click on "Partnering with Your Community" to find out about various community service projects. Additionally, at least once during the semester, the ELP participants submit a weekly reflective journal through Your Portfolio, describing their leadership efforts in organizing their community service project. Recording this information enables participants to see gaps in their backgrounds better and illuminates areas that need to be explored further.

A recent ELP graduate, Kyle, benefited from his involvement with the USC Leadership Model. In his first year, Kyle was involved in the Emerging Leader Program. He utilized this experience to springboard into a plethora of co-curricular activities. Kyle was asked to represent the student's perspective on a variety of university initiatives including "Your Portfolio." During his junior year he approached the coordinator of the USC Volunteer Center about the feasibility of creating a Homelessness/Spirituality Alternative Spring Break Program. The Dean of Religious Life had also approached this same coordinator about a similar idea. The coordinator introduced Kyle to the Dean of Religious Life. They conducted a week of intense activities with the migrant worker community in the Monterey Bay area and continued the project back in Los Angeles with the Dome Village Project. Kyle's leadership ability was challenged throughout this entire process. This experience encouraged him to question his values and beliefs constantly.

Interdisciplinary Leadership

To further USC's integrated approach to leadership, Student Affairs staff have initiated conversations with faculty to develop an interdisciplinary minor in leadership. The academic base will be the Philosophy Department. Contributing departments include History, International Relations, English, Sociology, Business, Cinema/TV, and Communication. The objective of the minor is for students to acquire a broad-based understanding of leadership, from multiple disciplines, grounded in a philosophical framework. Students will be required to take an introductory course, called a gateway course, in the Philosophy Department designed to acquaint students with the fundamental issues of leadership and introduce them to the concepts and techniques necessary for independent thinking leading to a broadening of perspectives about leadership. They will choose then from classes grouped in the following categories: philosophical and historical foundations in leadership, personal and social competence in leadership, case studies in leadership, leadership in a national context, and leadership in an international context. For example, after taking the gateway course, a student may choose a course on leadership and ethics, followed by a course on world political leadership and a course called "The Art and Adventure of Leadership."

Non-Credit Courses

As mentioned earlier in the chapter, community outreach is critical to USC's mission. The final leadership initiative example described in this chapter is a non-credit bearing course titled, "Critical Issues in Race, Class, and Leadership in Education" (CIRCLE). This course embraces ethical, transnational/multi-ethnic and systemic perspectives. CIRCLE is taught by the current Director of Asian Pacific American Student Services and a Los Angeles Unified School District teacher. There are three objectives for this class: (1) to introduce the Asian Pacific American community-based perspectives on issues; (2) to analyze critically the concept of leadership through the rubric of community and society progress; and (3) to enable individuals seeking leadership impact to network with one another. Community outreach includes visits to the Thai Community Development Center and the Asian Pacific American Legal Center.

Midway through the semester, USC CIRCLE students hold a joint retreat with their University of California Los Angeles counterpart group. The retreat provides an opportunity for students to discuss their similar interests and concerns. As one participant stated, "CIRCLE is a great eye-opening experience for students of all backgrounds at USC." As a result of taking this class one Cambodian student recognized the lack of involvement of Cambodian students and eventually founded the United Cambodian Student Association.

SUMMARY

We believe USC is a model urban laboratory for teaching and learning about leadership. USC's location on the Pacific Rim gives us hope and excitement in designing student affairs programs, which can thrive in a networked, knowledge era. This chapter has discussed the differences between emerging and traditional leadership paradigms and has outlined some of the ways in which these new leadership paradigms can inform the programs we design for students to encourage them to embrace non-hierarchical leadership strategies. In a networked, knowledge era leadership takes on relational and non-hierarchical characteristics. In today's world each and every person has the ability to influence change. Our society will continue to change rapidly in the new millennium, and we are proud to produce leaders to influence global change.

REFERENCES

Bloland, P. A., Stamatakos, L. C., & Rogers, R. R. (1994). *Reform in student affairs.* Greensboro, NC: ERIC.

Bok, D. (1988). Ethics, the university & society. *Harvard Magazine, 90*(5), 39–50.

Capra, F. (1992). Changes in management—management of change: The systemic approach. *World Business Academy Perspectives, 6*(3).

Chickering, A. W., & Reisser, L. (1993). *Education and identity* (2nd ed.). San Francisco: Jossey-Bass.

The Chronicle of Higher Education. (1999, August 27). *The Almanac issue* [Special issue], *46*(1), 29.

Gilligan, C. (1977). In a different voice: Women's conceptions of the self and of morality. *Harvard Educational Review, 47*(4), 481–517.

Komives, S. R., Lucas, N., & McMahon, T. R. (1998). *Exploring leadership: For college students who want to make a difference.* San Francisco: Jossey-Bass.

Matusak, L. 1997. *Finding your voice: Learning to lead—anywhere you want to make a difference.* San Francisco: Jossey-Bass.

Perry, W. G., Jr. (1981). Cognitive and ethical growth: The making of meaning. In A. Chickering (Ed.), *The modern American college.* San Francisco: Jossey-Bass.

Senge, P. (1996, November). Learning organizations: The promise and the possibilities. *The Systems Thinker, 7*(9).

Wheatley, M. J. (1992). *Leadership and the new science: Learning about organization from an orderly universe.* San Francisco: Berrett-Koehler.

Chapter 12

Learning and Leading:
A Class Project Provides Context

Nancy S. Huber

Perhaps the highest hope that we hold for students as they leave institutions of higher learning is that they become contributing members of their communities. That community may be a rural town, a neighborhood, a workplace, a metropolis, an organization, a national government body, or a multinational corporation. Whatever the nature of the community, what its members have in common is a shared responsibility for creating their collective future and contributing to the higher purpose of their communities. To fulfill their roles effectively as community leaders, students must be lifelong learners. Is higher education providing a broad enough range of opportunities for students to be engaged in learning and leading? This chapter first outlines the development of a non-hierarchical approach to leadership at the University of Arizona, then discusses the implementation of this approach through the use of the curricular model known as "Leadership Concepts and Contexts."

As an associate professor with responsibility for teaching upper-division courses and working with graduate students at the University of Arizona, the above question on leadership opportunities for students is important to me. It is perhaps more compelling because of my previous experience as an educator in the field of community leadership development. With this chapter, I outline the development of a non-hierarchical leadership course and discuss the implementation of this approach through the use of the Leadership Concepts and Contexts curricular model.

TRADITIONAL OPPORTUNITIES ARE AVAILABLE

The University of Arizona (UA) in Tucson is a large, public research institution and Arizona's land grant university. There are a number of ways that UA students can be elected or appointed to positions that afford the opportunity to learn leadership skills. These positional leadership roles are derived from traditional activities that may be found on many campuses. Examples from student government, intercollegiate sports, the intramural program, Greek social organizations, and hundreds of campus clubs suggest a multitude of opportunities available for students to be leaders. In fact there are more than four hundred chances to be elected or appointed to a leadership position. However, on a campus the size of the University of Arizona, the reality is that only about 1% of the student population hold these leadership positions. What about the remaining 33,500 students? Who decides who leads? If we limit the preparation of leaders to those who are duly elected, appointed by someone in authority, hired for a managerial job, or in some way named to a leadership position, then we do a disservice to all the potential leaders who go out into the world with a degree but with neither experience nor expectation about their role as leader.

LEARNING AND LEADING

The design of the Leadership Concepts and Contexts course has evolved over a number of years. Recently, the incorporation of a class project became the focal point of the semester course. Students understand that they are expected to be leading, not simply learning about those who have been labeled "leader." Although much of this is accomplished through students' class projects, the overall design of the course includes a variety of experiential learning activities. For this reason, the class meets once a week for an extended session. From my experience as instructor, this extended session is eminently more useful than trying to squeeze concepts and practice into more frequent but shorter class periods. In addition, it allows for students to interact more and to begin to build community in the classroom. I also limit the size of the class so that we can sit in a circle and talk face-to-face. Actual lecture time is held to the barest minimum. Topics covered each semester include:

• A personal look at leadership;
• The meaning of leadership;
• A reason for leading;
• The context for leading;
• A personal philosophy of leadership;
• Leaders, stakeholders, and followers;
• Building community;
• Leading and lifelong learning;
• Being a leader.

Two class sessions late in the semester are devoted to skill-building and are derived from the context of the class project. In addition, students are asked to interview at least one leader and complete outside reading assignments. One or two sessions are set aside for the class project and presentation. The text for Leadership Concepts and Contexts is one I developed specifically to support the philosophy and methods used. It is grounded in the belief that leadership occurs when people care enough about a situation to want to engage others in bringing about positive change. Additionally, the book provides guidelines for creating a context within which students can be leaders rather than merely study how others lead.

Students in the course participate in several foundational activities to prepare themselves for the eventual selection and implementation of an appropriate project. Self-discovery and disclosure are the focus of early sessions. For example, the first time we meet, I ask each student to make a name tent to use while we are getting to know each other. In addition to their name, I ask them to draw a symbol that tells us something about who they are. As we go around the room with introductions, they not only get past the hurdle of speaking in front of the class for the first time, they begin the process of building relationships that are important as we create a sense of community in the classroom. This activity sets the tone for lively discussion in class and makes it apparent that each student is expected to contribute by participating actively.

Each class session includes some type of experience-based learning activity. There are suggested activities listed at the end of each chapter in the text. Some are designed to be done outside the classroom, but many of them are incorporated into the course session. The informal classroom setting, the extended class time with minimal lecture, and the hands-on learning all contribute to engaging the students in *doing* leadership rather than *studying* leadership. In addition to creating a climate in which course participants know and feel comfortable with each other, I encourage self-exploration activities designed to assist students in understanding themselves as leaders.

Perhaps the biggest challenge and the most rewarding learning experience comes from the design and implementation of the class project. This is not something that I assign to students. Rather, the process of choosing the project and then figuring out how to do it is an end in itself. Generally, there are only two parameters for the class project: everyone must be involved, and the project must engage and enhance the campus community. Although actual project outcomes vary, they are not trivial. Several have resulted in web site creation and may be found on-line at http://www.u.arizona.edu/~nhuber/classes.html. Students' reflections have pointed out that the project is THE learning experience.

Along with critical thinking skills (i.e., the analysis and synthesis of data essential to the implementation of their project), reflective thinking is not only espoused but woven into the fabric of the course. Writing in a journal is the primary reflection tool. When the class meets for the first time, I point out why keeping a journal is important: it is an effective way for students to track their learning; it is a way to react to what happens in class; and it can help them to make connections between events or activities and the concepts we discuss. I also point out that I will underscore my belief in the benefits of keeping a journal by providing ten minutes at the end of each class for them to reflect and write. (And while they write in their journals, I write in mine, too.) As further encouragement of reflective thinking and writing, I schedule two one-on-one appointments during the semester to talk with them about their journals—not to read and criticize them, but to discuss the process—whether it is working for them, and if they discovered any "aha's" when they looked back through their notes prior to the scheduled appointment.

Typically, students report a significant deepening in their reflective writing between the first and second journal discussion appointment. Early in the course, it is as though they feel a need to write for me or to somehow "do it right" until after we have a chance to just talk about the *process* of keeping a journal and what it can mean to them. I see journals as an important tool in developing meaning-making skills. Drath and Palus (1994) refer to meaning-making as "constructing knowledge of ourselves and the world" (p. 2). Drath (1996) writes "Leadership is being created by people making sense and meaning of their work together, and this process, in turn, can bring leaders into being" (p. 2). For me, meaning-making goes beyond research and reflection to capture the intuitive essence of the leadership relationship. When people come together to create shared meaning, they are building community.

THE EVOLUTION OF LEADERSHIP CONCEPTS AND CONTEXTS

I was asked to create a leadership course at the University of Arizona because of my graduate training, my background in adult education program development, and my earlier success in the design and implementation of community leadership development programs. In my graduate training I discovered that we each have a personal philosophy of leadership that is uniquely our own, drawing on our experience as well as our core values and beliefs. When I studied with J. W. Apps, I began the lifelong process of discovering and honing my philosophical basis for both leadership and education (see Apps 1991, 1994). In addition, Apps introduced me to the work of Malcolm Knowles (1980), which underscores my role as a facilitator of learning rather than as the classroom authority. My work with volunteer leaders in communities and the non-profit sector evolved from many years of association with the Cooperative Extension Service as both a volunteer and a professional. Additionally, Bennett's *Reflections on Community Development Education* (1973) served as a source of some basic principles concerning helping to move a community through conflict to compromise and, ultimately, to collaboration.

There are, however, distinct differences between the community setting and the classroom that are important to consider when designing a college course. When I have been asked to come into a community or organization to enhance local leadership capacity, the people with whom I work have a reason for wanting to be more effective leaders. In addition, they had knowledge of the context within which they wanted to bring about positive change. In the classroom, however, students sign up for the leadership course from curiosity or to fulfill a requirement. My early experience teaching an experimental course was minimally successful because there was neither a common purpose nor a shared context within which to apply concepts and skills. Without purpose and context, students were *studying* leaders rather than *becoming* leaders.

Learning and leading go hand in hand. People rarely learn how to be leaders before accepting the role. Leadership is not so much a position as it is a way of being in the world—a propensity for action grounded in personal passion which provides a purpose for leading. Exploring the context of that purpose is part of the learning process, as is learning how to collaborate effectively with others. Acquiring and honing skills to be applied in bringing about the intended change becomes more relevant once the context is understood. I caution against teaching skills and concepts in isolation without some relevant application and experience because it promulgates the notion that once you have the "toolbox" and the title, then you are a leader. I assure students that they will not need to learn all the concepts and master every leadership skill before they become leaders. Indeed, this is why collaborative leadership is so successful—no one needs to know everything!

NEW WAYS TO THINK ABOUT LEADERSHIP

We need to think broadly about what leading means. As a returning adult student in the early 1980s, my intent was to learn about the role volunteers play in society and find ways to apply adult education theory to volunteer development programs. What I discovered was that another word for volunteer was leader. When someone cares enough about a situation or a community to want to make it better, that person is ready to volunteer to lead. This new awareness altered forever the conventional view of leadership I had espoused for decades; leaders are the bosses, the people with position and title, and those who are elected to lofty office.

One way to move beyond the stereotypical view of leadership is to accept the notion that there may not be one singular and entirely discreet definition of leadership that will stand the test of time and the rigors of research. In the classroom, students' exploration of what leadership means on a personal level is a powerful way to underscore the validity of non-hierarchical leadership. In *Leading from Within: Developing Personal Direction* (Huber, 1998, p. 26), I state my reluctance to define leadership for others. Instead, I share what leadership means to me: "Leadership is a shared responsibility for creating a better world in which to live and work. It is manifested in our passion to engage others in bringing about purposeful change." This assertion comes from the belief that we are all called to lead. Additionally, it is based on the assumption that leading and managing are not the same—different but not dissociated. In general, managers produce a degree of predictability and order, while leaders produce change, often to a dramatic degree (Bennis, 1989; Conger, 1992). This is not to say that good managers are ineffective leaders or that outstanding leaders do not need some management skills.

In higher education institutions, leadership is studied within several contexts— business schools, human resource development, colleges of education, student services, and the social sciences to name merely a few. Rost (1991) explored leadership definitions and came to the conclusion that "in the 1990s, the concept of leadership does not add up because leadership scholars and practitioners have no definition of leadership to hold on to" (p. 8). He claims further that without a universally accepted definition, "scholars do not know what it is they are studying and practitioners do not know what it is that they are doing" (p. 8). These statements underscore my belief that the push for a universal definition of leadership is intended to provide a standard for researchers to use in measuring and quantifying what it is that the people they see as leaders have in common. However, a research model may not be the best way to understand what leading actually entails. There are, for example, a number of ways to lead that do not fit traditional organizational research models that were developed with a view of the world which mirrors Newtonian physics—linear, reductive, isolated, hierarchical. However, I believe we need to move away from this "either/or" frame of reference to embrace a "both/and" mind set. This new approach is consistent with the more current post-industrial view of leadership and organizational change—non-linear, creative, contextual, non-hierarchical. This perspective espouses a number of ways to lead that have become increasingly popular and substantially effective (Senge, 1990; Wheatley, 1994). (See Cherrey and Allen [Chapter 5 in this volume] for a discussion of the importance of connectivity within the post-industrial leadership paradigm.)

Collaborative leadership describes a way of leading in which responsibility for bringing about positive change is shared among the various members of a community, group, or organization (Chrislip & Larson, 1994; Komives, 1996). This mode of leading recognizes that power shared *with* people and resources is more effective than trying to gain power *over* them. When leadership is shared in this manner, a wide array of skills, ideas, and perspectives can be brought to bear on an issue to serve the common good. Everyone has something to contribute. The notion of followers as passive and in need of constant direction is discarded. Rather than expecting to be told what to do, people are prepared and ready to step in when their particular talent is needed.

Like Greenleaf (1991, 1996), I believe leadership and service go hand in hand. Serving a higher cause, serving the best interests of our community, serving others who can be made more whole by our willingness to collaborate—this is what being a leader means. Larry Spears, CEO of the Greenleaf Center for Servant Leadership has said, "Servant leaders have a common purpose—to replace competition with community. Servant leadership is a walk of faith by which leaders and followers are not changed or adjusted, but transformed. It is grounded in a way of leading which, rather than telling people what to do, gives meaning to what they are already doing" (1995). Greenleaf's philosophy is one which pervades my role as a leadership educator.

Concomitant with the notion that a perfect leadership definition has not been developed, I have come to believe that there is no perfect leadership model from which to teach. Many are either too prescriptive, too research oriented, too corporate focused, too much management-in-disguise-of-leadership based, or just too "cute" (designed to market books or workshops). For me, particularly in my work with students, I see great value in encouraging them to find or build a personal model—one that means something to the individual. The course content has evolved over the years as I have focused more on leadership concepts and much less on management techniques. More recently, my teaching draws on collaborative leadership principles (Chrislip & Larson, 1994; Komives, 1996) and Greenleaf's concepts of servant leadership (1991, 1996), and it aligns with the Social Change Model of Leadership Development (Higher Education Research Institute [HERI], 1996).

Starting with the basic assumptions that leading is concerned with bringing about positive change (Bennis, 1989), and that leadership is a relationship (Kouzes & Posner, 1987), I have developed a simple model designed to encourage students to see themselves as leaders. I ask them to complete the following sentence: Leadership for _____ with _____. The first blank is about passion and purpose while the second recognizes that there are other leaders, followers, and stakeholders who will be part of the process of bringing about intended change. Together, the reason for wanting to bring about positive change and the people who will be involved in or affected by it comprise the context within which leadership occurs. When purpose is clear and people within the change context have been identified and engaged, then the particular skills to be learned or honed become apparent.

BUILDING COMMUNITY ON CAMPUS

Perhaps the most profound lesson students learn in the course of developing and implementing a class project is the discovery that the class becomes, in essence, a community. About two-thirds of the way through the semester, tempers flare, conflict arises, heels dig in, the project threatens to fall apart, and I hear statements such as "We'll never agree! Why don't you just tell us what to do—you're the professor." Then there is always the class that I call the "turnaround session" where compromises are made in the interest of getting the project done. Things fall into place and another terrific project comes to fruition. This prompts a discussion of the four stages of community—forming, storming, norming, and performing (Gozdz, 1995). Drawing from Tuckman's (1965) work on group development, Gozdz describes the four stages as follows: Forming, or pseudo-community, is characterized by polite behavior and dependence on decisions made by someone in charge. Storming is the stage in which chaos emerges, conflicts erupt, and emotions run high. Norming occurs once differences are out in the open and group cohesiveness replaces competition. Performing is the stage of authentic communication, acknowledgment of differences, and commitment to the larger goal. Reflecting on the normal behavior that has occurred in the classroom elicits some "aha's" and the knowledge gained from students' own experience is transferred to deeper understanding about why the campus community might behave the way it does. This, in turn, strengthens their desire to have a positive influence on their academic community through accomplishing the goals of their project.

Why the focus on campus community? We are in a time when the spotlight on higher education has illuminated the need for the institution to be more relevant and less arrogant, to be connected to our greater community rather than isolated within our departmental boundaries, to be student-centered rather than preoccupied with disseminating knowledge. Those institutions that are heavily funded with public monies are under pressure to be more broadly responsive to the needs and issues of concern to the citizenry. External resource providers (e.g., the W. K. Kellogg Foundation and Pew Charitable Trust) are calling for and investing in the transformation of higher education. This transformation is more than the aggregate of incremental changes at the margin of individual administrative units and departments. It is more than developing a new policy manual, more than a flashy new logo or an administratively driven, politically correct vision statement.

Transformation will not come about until the campus community becomes integrated in the pursuit of the educational enterprise—teaching, research, outreach and service—which blurs discipline boundaries. The transformation of higher education will not become a reality unless or until the student experience is transformed, and students will help us understand how to do that—if we ask them. In much the same way that it takes a community to raise a child, it takes a campus community to educate a student. I believe the student role in building a sense of campus community is essential. When students realize that they are part of a larger community, I believe they will step up to their responsibility (and their right) to be involved in bringing about the changes that will truly transform the university. Thus, the context for each class project is found in the campus community.

SUMMARY

Leadership development efforts sponsored by many student affairs units in higher education are intended in general to meet the needs of those students seeking positional leadership roles in campus clubs, organizations, and sports. In some cases leadership development programs are co-curricular and linked to a certification process. However, to prepare students fully to take their place as collaborative leaders contributing to the well-being of the communities in which they will live and work once they graduate, non-hierarchical leadership education must become part of the academic mission. Course offerings that provide a means to incorporate leadership learning and practice in a meaningful context can reach students outside the mainstream of traditional programs targeting elected and appointed student leaders. The course described here provides an example of leadership development which is built on the belief that leadership is a collaborative effort grounded in the desire to both create and serve community. Class projects undertaken by students in Leadership Concepts and Contexts provide a context for learning and a service to the campus community.

REFERENCES

Apps, J. W. (1991). *Mastering the teaching of adults*. Malabar, FL: Krieger.

Apps, J. W. (1994). *Leadership for the emerging age: Transforming practice in adult and continuing education*. San Francisco: Jossey-Bass.

Bennett, A. E. (1973). *Reflections on community development education*. University Park, PA: The Pennsylvania State University, Northeast Regional Center for Rural Development.

Bennis, W. (1989). *Why leaders can't lead*. San Francisco: Jossey-Bass.

Chrislip, D., & Larson, C. (1994). *Collaborative leadership*. San Francisco: Jossey-Bass.

Conger, J. A. (1992). *Learning to lead: The art of transforming managers into leaders*. San Francisco: Jossey-Bass.

Drath, W. H. (1996). Changing our minds about leadership. *Issues and Observations, 16*(1), 1–4.

Drath, W. H., & Palus, C. J. (1994). *Making common sense: Leadership as meaning-making in a community of practice*. Greensboro, NC: Center for Creative Leadership.

Gozdz, K. (1995). Building a core competence in community. *The Systems Thinker, 6*(2), 8–12.

Greenleaf, R. K. (1991). *The servant as leader*. Indianapolis: The Robert K. Greenleaf Center.

Greenleaf, R. K. (1996). *On becoming a servant leader*. San Francisco: Jossey-Bass.

Higher Education Research Institute. (1996). *A Social Change Model of Leadership Development* (3rd ed.). Los Angeles: Author.

Huber, N. S. (1998). *Leading from within: Developing personal direction*. Malabar, FL: Krieger.

Knowles, M. (1980). *The modern practice of adult education*. Chicago: Follett.

Komives, S. R. (1996, July/August). A call for collaborative leadership. *About Campus*, 2–3.

Kouzes, J., & Posner, B. (1987). *The leadership challenge: How to get extraordinary things done in organizations*. San Francisco: Jossey-Bass.

Rost, J. C. (1991). *Leadership for the twenty-first century*. New York: Praeger.

Senge, P. M. (1990). *The fifth discipline: The art and practice of the learning organization*. New York: Doubleday.

Spears, L. (1995, October 19). *Soul of leadership*. Remarks presented at a conference sponsored by the Greenleaf Center, Indianapolis, IN.

ORGANIZATIONAL CHANGE WITHIN HIGHER EDUCATION

Kerr (1995) noted that "[the] modern university [is] a 'pluralistic' institution—pluralistic in several senses: in having several purposes, not one; in having several centers of power, not one; in serving several clienteles, not one" (p. 103). Birnbaum (1988) stated that governance and management within higher education must contend with multiple sources of control, unclear or competing missions, decentralized structure, and constrained resources. Hull, Hunter, and Kuh (1983) comment that student affairs organizations defy explanation as simply or ideally bureaucratic. They propose that multiple perspectives—"Bureaucratic, loose coupling, incentive exchange, or organized anarchy . . . [provide] a complete view of what goes on in a student affairs organization" (p. 35). Allen (1990) described the environment of American higher education as inherently unpredictable, turbulent and chaotic: "Organizations are seen as riding on the waves of change and existing within an environment of permanent white water" (p. 57). Within this "white water," pressure for change and natural processes of evolution continue.

Perhaps the greatest fear of anyone currently pursuing or about to undertake a change effort is that there will be resistance. The existence of multiple power bases within higher education means that resistance can come from the top, or from anywhere within the organization, and can take many forms. During the change effort, Dartmouth's professional residential life staff experienced resistance from its student staff in three ways. Verbal resistance was vocalized disagreement (complaints, or efforts to dissuade) with the change process. Students working alone or collectively to undermine the change process through intentional action or in-action demonstrated functional resistance. Finally, philosophical resistance presented as disagreement that change was needed and differences of opinion as to the direction of the change effort.

ORGANIZATIONAL CHANGE AT DARTMOUTH COLLEGE: A CASE STUDY

Dartmouth is a private, Ivy League institution of approximately 4,000 undergraduate and 1,000 graduate students located in the small New England town of Hanover, New Hampshire. In 1983 the Dartmouth College Board of Trustees voted to establish an Office of Residential Life. With this decision, which was informed by discussions with students, parents, administrators, faculty, and alumni/ae, the Board of Trustees sought to address inconsistencies between the quality of students' residential and academic experiences. For much of its history, the college had served students in residence by merely issuing keys at the beginning of the year and expecting the return of those keys at the end of the year. There were no support structures, no common area spaces, and no central management for planning or evaluation.

Within a year of the Board of Trustees' decision, the Office of Residential Life began to "encourage the integration of the intellectual and social lives of students . . . [by establishing] . . . residential and social opportunities created to enhance and encourage the primary educational goals of the College" (Kastan, 1982, p. 2). At the same time, the professional staff worked to create new cultural norms by promoting the idea that a strong residential life program was essential to the development of college students. Thus, during the first thirteen years, the office successfully developed a general blueprint for residential education, criteria, and processes for selecting and training staff; added student and professional staff; and improved the physical environment within each residence hall. With the creation of programming councils, resident students became active participants in the residential community.

By the fall of 1995 there had been a complete changeover of professional staff in the residential life program. Two new Area Directors were hired and the Assistant Dean position had become vacant and would remain so for an entire year. While this instability suggested possibilities for new energy and ideas, the new Area Directors found a residential program that had evolved significantly during its short history and lingering issues that required immediate attention. Student staff members were unclear about their role within the residential life program. While the exact cause of their confusion was difficult to identify, it manifested as over-dependence on individual interpretations of program philosophy and goals, fear of innovation, and role confusion. Student staff complained of being ill-prepared and ill-supported by professional staff. Moreover, the program had begun to stagnate due to the lack of commitment and creative energy so often contributed by student staff.

Because student and professional staff members were unhappy with the state of the program, there was consensus that something needed to change. Operating with the assumption that successful change requires collaboration between student and professional staff (an assumption which has since been supported by Komives, Lucas, & McMahon, 1998) and that collaboration produces superior outcomes (Robertson, 1987), the professional staff sought a process that could best establish a collective vision for the future. The SCM seemed ideal for this task. In the winter of 1996, members of the undergraduate and professional staff began working collaboratively to develop a curriculum for the residential program.

Centered around seven, interconnected core values known as the Seven Cs, the SCM asserts the primacy of the process of leadership over position and "emphasize[s] clarification of values, the development of self-awareness, trust and the capacity to listen and serve others, and through collaborative work to bring about change for the common good" (HERI, 1996, p. 11). The professional staff believed that use of the SCM would:

- enable professional and student staff to become partners in the effort to determine a vision for the residential life program;

• give voice to student staff concerns and harness their creative energy; and

• allow the change team to define guiding values for the residential program before articulating them in a formal curriculum.

The Social Change Model in Action

A change team of nine volunteer students and two professional staff was convened in the winter of 1996 to develop a residential curriculum for the Office of Residential Life. All student staff members had been invited to participate in the effort. The effort to develop the curriculum required nearly a year of bi-weekly meetings featuring reflection, dialogue, and consensual decision making.

A member of the professional staff, who had previously experienced a change effort guided by the SCM, served as the primary facilitator for Dartmouth's change team. The students were given copies of the SCM Guidebook, version II and asked to read selected pages. The professional staff imagined that like past experiences, this would produce a rich discussion of the Model, its role in the change effort, and the responsibilities of each team member. Unexpectedly, discussion was limited. The students claimed to need no clarification of the SCM but were intrigued and willing to use the Model to guide the change process. Admittedly, the lack of lively dialogue raised concerns about whether the students had actually read the guidebook. Yet when probed further, the student staff could describe the values of the Model and argued that the values were "simply common sense," or "things [we] normally do when working with groups." Because these responses seemed to indicate that the students had read the materials, the professional staff made the decision to move forward. The professional staff believed that true engagement of the SCM depended upon how the process was facilitated. With effective facilitation, the students could learn the Model as they practiced it and overcome any shortcomings brought on by the limited, initial discussion.

Facilitation. To generate open and honest dialogue among team members, the professional staff worked to abandon any perception of "adult" control of the change process. To this end, professional staff members restricted their role to facilitation—asking questions which drew out members' thoughts, feelings and perceptions of the residential environment, sharing information, offering observations about process, and contributing information about practices at other institutions for consideration.

It is important to note that responsibility for facilitating the change process was not shared by all team members. The professional staff created and facili-tated each of the practices designed to engage the team in using the SCM. This dependence upon the professional staff as facilitators required particular dili-gence to assure that all vestiges of "adult" control were abandoned in favor of collaborative action. Admittedly, greater attention to discussion and practice of the SCM might have enabled all team members to share equally in the role of facilitator, and it is possible that not sharing this role was one way the professional staff exerted some level of unconscious control. Because the language and spirit of the Model—terms such as "collaboration," "citizenship," and "controversy with civility"—was evident during team discussions, it seems that the group dynamic was not harmed. Further, the use of these terms suggests that while the students may not have understood the details of the SCM, they did appreciate and attempt to operate within it.

Commitment. The change team chose to schedule a regular team meeting time and location. Team members also received regular reminders of meetings and minutes via e-mail. Yet, because each team member expressed personal motivations for being involved in the change project (as will be elaborated below), there was a high level of commitment to the project. For example, during a brief hiatus in the team's work in the spring quarter to conduct the annual staff selection process, team members continued to stay in contact with the professional staff to secure guarantees that the change effort would continue. Other than those students (approximately four of the nine) whose enrollment patterns did not allow them to remain with the project, each team member remained involved until completion.

Reflection and Dialogue. A systematic process of reflection and dialogue allowed team members to uncover and express thoughts and feelings consistently. For example, at the earliest team meetings each member was invited to reflect upon and share his or her motivations for becoming involved in the change effort. The professional staff shared frustrations with the program and observations of the student staff's role confusion. The student staff were honest (if not blunt) about their frustrations with the residential life program and initial changes made by the professional staff. Without exception, the students shared a strong desire to make things better. These challenging discussions helped identify common ground and shared values that informed the emerging residential curriculum.

Subsequent meetings focused on team members sharing values and activities they believed should undergird the residential program. This focus took the form of sharing personal experiences, anecdotes, conversations with students and staff members, observations about the residential experience, ideas, wish lists, or anything members felt had bearing on the evolving curriculum. After several meetings, a clear picture began to emerge of the components and structure of the curriculum.

Recording. At each meeting, a member of the change team took notes. The professional staff held this responsibility initially, which provided the opportunity to listen effectively and demonstrate a willingness to really hear students' opinions. The notes were developed into minutes and distributed to all team members via e-mail. Having a written record facilitated group reflection and dialogue. Each team meeting opened with a review of the minutes and the opportunity to generate feedback on previous discussion points.

Disagreement. Use of the SCM introduced the idea that disagreement is an integral and valuable aspect of group work. Permission to disagree encouraged team members to share opinions honestly and work through conflicts. Ironically, there were few real disagreements. An example of how disagreement was commonly experienced and managed by the team came during the attempt to name the components of the residential curriculum. One student proposed naming the curriculum areas after each of the seven values within the SCM. When that effort failed to satisfy all members of the team, another student proposed naming the curriculum areas such that each began with the letter "C" as a way of paying homage to the Model. When that effort failed also, the group suggested that at least each area begin with the same letter of the alphabet. Although disagreements and long periods of silence characterized this discussion, the team remained committed to working through the difficulty. As trust grew, consensus was easier to achieve.

At times, the relationship among team members seemed symbiotic. It was startling to witness how ideas struggling to find articulation in one team member would find voice in another. For example, during a discussion of staff roles and responsibilities, the professional staff worried that issues of holding students accountable for misbehavior and establishing community norms would be neglected. This performance expectation had not been clearly expressed by the Office of Residential Life, and the student staff performed this responsibility inconsistently. Just as one anxious, professional staff member attempted to offer this item for discussion, a student insisted that it be added to the list of responsibilities being deliberated.

Sharing. The change team endeavored to engage many stakeholders in the effort to create the residential curriculum. This meant that all student staff members were invited to participate in the change effort. While nine participated actively, at least two staff members expressed interest but were unable to attend meetings. These members received minutes via e-mail and were asked to share thoughts and feedback in a similar fashion. Any feedback offered was disseminated at team meetings.

Those members who attended meetings were asked to focus on the needs of the community being served (i.e., resident students). Thus team members were asked to reflect upon and share observations regarding resident student behavior, trends, and attitudes before brainstorming curriculum areas or staff roles. Team members were invited to share the group's efforts with resident students, other student staff members, professional staff members across campus, friends at other institutions, and so on. Unfortunately, this student-led sharing was successful only to a limited degree, and so the change team benefited only from input gained by the professional staff from colleagues within and outside Dartmouth.

Once the curriculum was in a cohesive form, a proposal comprising the curriculum and reflections on the change process was written by all members. The entire team presented the curriculum at a meeting of professional and student staff members within the Office of Residential Life. All team members took responsibility for presenting the curriculum and answering questions. This discussion enabled further refinement of the curriculum.

OUTCOMES

Perhaps the most significant and durable outcome of the change effort has been the creation of the residential co-curriculum. The curriculum has two components—the first outlines educational objectives for the residential community while the second defines the various roles that student staff employ to accomplish those objectives. The curriculum contributed to the evolving culture of the residential program by codifying program goals and staff performance expectations. The curriculum is printed in all staff manuals and selection materials. During candidate information sessions and staff training, the students learn how they are meant to work within the residential community. Thus the curriculum guides the work of all staff, communicates the residential program's values, and perpetuates the organizational culture established during the change process.

Another benefit of utilizing the SCM was that it improved communication and trust, transforming the relationship between professional and student staff from one of resistance and antagonism. According to Certo (1985), resistance to change is the result of fear. The SCM process created a forum where student and professional staff could expose and address fears. Embracing open communication led to the discovery that student and professional staff shared similar frustrations and aspirations. This challenged initial presumptions that the student and professional staff must be adversaries.

The shift we experienced in student-professional staff interaction and the new residential curriculum marked a new spirit of cooperation in which the professional staff now involve students intentionally and regularly in much of the decision making and planning of office programs and procedures. The opportunity to make a lasting contribution to the residential program (couched within an environment of expressed trust, respect, and expectations of excellence) has inspired many student staff members to be integrally involved in the residential program. When staff are asked to volunteer, or selected to participate in special projects or committees, students are more likely to volunteer and give a great deal of themselves—demonstrating a strong sense of ownership for the program. To encourage this growing interest, a departmental committee structure was created to involve students in planning and implementing annual staff selection and training processes. Student staff members now hire student staff, represent the residential program at meetings, and plan major departmental events successfully. Each year eight to ten incoming and returning staff members determine the number, content, and scheduling of the training program. Some present training sessions.

It is worth noting that perhaps the only drawback that greater student involvement has wrought is that sometimes it becomes difficult for students to negotiate appropriate boundaries. Some students become so invested that they view themselves as professional staff. When this has occurred, it has harmed their ability to balance their obligations as students, hurt relationships with peers and professional staff, and led them to make unilateral decisions for which they felt they had authority, but were ill-informed. In response, the professional staff has learned to embrace the SCM process to engage the staff member(s) in dialogue. These follow up conversations include reflection on mutual expectations for the working relationship (boundaries and where support can be offered), a willingness to embrace the source of the conflict that arose, and a commitment to work through conflict towards consensus and greater understanding. This method has helped to resolve conflict and reinforce the trusting and respectful relationships between student and professional staff.

Utilizing the SCM was both challenging and rewarding. We found that group decision making, collaboration, consensus, and attention to process required significant time and focus. Initial meetings did not consider what was to be changed or a vision for the curriculum, but focused instead on personal reflection and defining the process for working together. This slower and more methodical pace can be difficult to sustain when the environment requires or emphasizes immediate outcomes. Yet, it should be noted that while the process may have compromised efficiency, it did generate a high quality product and a new organizational culture which otherwise would not have been achieved. The newly developed residential curriculum is a wonderful synthesis of the ideas and values of each member of the change team and the communities on whose behalf it was created.

A second challenge to utilizing the SCM may simply be a matter of perception, but is worthy of discussion. For the professional staff, working with the SCM at times felt like a loss of control over the residential program. The professional staff needed to confront their perceptions that their experience, training, and organizational perspective afforded them the best vision of the need and direction for change. These convictions made it difficult at times to trust the students and process. Similarly, those who facilitate a change process using the SCM will need to demonstrate honesty and self-restraint to abandon personal preferences regarding the direction of the change effort and instead focus attention on the facilitator role and engaging others as equal partners. If authority is shared effectively, it may be striking how the ideas and values of those engaged in the change process will converge into a collective voice. Little "successes" throughout the change process will make it easier to abandon fears concerning control and trust.

Attention to the self-reflective aspects of SCM may aid in addressing the challenge of loss of control. Awareness of individual strengths and weaknesses regarding flexibility, ambiguity, and adaptability, as well as overall group dynamics, may be explored through discussion and/or measures such as the Myers-Briggs Type Indicator. Awareness of individual preferences may help individuals to become more comfortable with the process and promise of the SCM.

What We Learned

Involve Those Affected by the Change. At Dartmouth, the student staff should have been involved in the discussions and efforts at change much earlier. Had the student staff been engaged in the change effort from the very beginning, a trusting, collaborative staff culture would have been created much sooner. Once the student staff did become involved in the change project, resistance on their part decreased significantly. This shift in the overall group dynamic happened not only because individual fears were addressed through discussion, but also because the effort demonstrated to the entire student staff a commitment from the professional staff to invite, listen, and respond to student voices in decision making.

Communicate Openly and Consistently. As noted above, regular, open discussion was an inherent feature of the change effort at Dartmouth. Consistent meetings sustained meaningful relationships among the change team characterized by a rich dialogue that allowed clear and common rationales for the curriculum to evolve. The process permitted members to disagree openly while seeking resolutions to conflicts that arose. As a result, the change team was able to uncover commonly held values and goals for the residential program and to overcome initial perceptions of one another as adversaries. Students and professional staff members developed mutual respect.

Remember Our Place within the Community. At times the SCM exacerbated the familiar tension between the desire to be collaborative and non-hierarchical within the process on the one hand, and professional roles and obligations within a hierarchical system on the other hand. Those who work with the SCM will need to be aware that it is a formidable task to create a truly power-neutral relationship with others (especially students) that is marked by honest communication while maintaining accountability to supervisors, protecting sensitive information, preserving professional ethics, and honoring institutional obligations. The effort will require a great deal of intentional planning and personal reflection. Facilitators will need to be conscious of and ready to set aside their biases and the urge to act independently of others. At Dartmouth, this required revisiting expectations concerning confidentiality to share sensitive information with the change team. Care may also need to be taken to educate colleagues and other organizational leaders about the SCM and its usefulness in bringing about effective, quality change.

Change by Non-Hierarchical Means Can Be Confusing. Once one is engaged in a truly open and collaborative change process, it will become clear that change by non-hierarchical means is messy. There may not be clear directives, someone to approve or guide the endeavor, or rules to follow. Often, there will be more questions raised than answered. At times, where the process is headed may be very unclear. However, the experience at Dartmouth revealed that trusting the process will yield a dynamic synthesis of ideas and values and a deeper level of understanding that will give birth to new levels of citizenship within the organization.

REFERENCES

Allen, K. E. (1990). Making sense out of chaos: Leading and living in dynamic systems. *Campus Activities Programming, 23*, 56–63.

Birnbaum, R. (1988). *How colleges work: The cybernetics of academic organization and leadership.* San Francisco: Jossey-Bass.

Certo, S. C. (1985). Fundamentals of changing an organization. In *Principles of modern management: Functions and systems* (3rd ed.). Dubuque, IA: William C. Brown.

Creamer, D. G., & Fredrick, P. M. (1991). Administrative and management theories: Tools for change. In T. K. Miller & R. B. Winston, Jr., et al. (Eds.), *Administration and leadership in student affairs: Actualizing student development in higher education* (pp. 134–157). Muncie, IN: Accelerated Development.

Higher Education Research Institute. (1996). *A Social Change Model of Leadership Development* (3rd ed.). Los Angeles: Author.

Hull, D. F., Hunter, D. E., & Kuh, G. D. (1983). Alternative perspectives on student affairs organizations. In G. D. Kuh (Ed.), *Understanding student affairs organizations* (pp. 27–37). San Francisco: Jossey-Bass.

Kastan, D. S. (1982). *Report of the committee on undergraduate life.* Hanover, NH: Dartmouth College.

Kerr, C. (1995). *The uses of the university* (4th ed.). Cambridge, MA: Harvard University Press.

Komives, S. R., Lucas, N., & McMahon, T. R. (1998). *Exploring leadership: For college students who want to make a difference.* San Francisco: Jossey-Bass.

Newman, F. (1998). The academy in transition: Lead or be led. *Liberal Education, 84*(2), 4–11.

Ramirez, B. C. (1993). Adapting to new student needs and characteristics. In M. J. Barr et al. (Eds.), *The handbook of student affairs administration* (pp. 427–438). San Francisco: Jossey-Bass.

Robertson, I. (1987). Social groups. In *Sociology* (3rd ed., pp. 167–189). New York: Worth Publishers.

Rudolph, F. (1990). *The American college and university: A history.* Athens: The University of Georgia Press.

Sanford, N. (1985). Some recollections of the free speech movement. *Journal of Counseling and Human Development, 64*, 14–18.

Chapter 18

The Advent of Leadership Development in the UCLA International Student Orientation Program

Mariana Zavala-Corzo

INTRODUCTION

The University of California, Los Angeles (UCLA) admits approximately 750 non-immigrant international students per year from over 100 countries to begin their undergraduate or graduate courses of study. These students, like their domestic counterparts, are exceptionally talented scholars and thinkers. Their scholastic achievements have placed them in elite circles among their peers, and international students have every reason to believe they will be successful during their tenure at UCLA.

Most of the international students arrive in Los Angeles in early September with a number of questions and concerns. Some wonder how they are going to find housing, secure bank accounts, and take other actions necessary to function in the community of Los Angeles. Others want information about the nature of the academic process and the intensity of the intellectual competitiveness awaiting them when the fall quarter begins at UCLA. Almost all new international students have concerns about establishing connections and making friends with other international and domestic students.

In effect, the new students are groping for answers to or assistance with a number of transitions they make as they leave their country with its familiar culture and engage in the culture of the United States. For more than twenty years staff members of the International Student Center (ISC) at UCLA have helped new international students with this transition by directly offering advice and guidance during their first few weeks at UCLA.

In recent years, a number of factors have prompted change in the ISC staff approach to Orientation. Most notably, the UCLA students who assist ISC staff with Orientation increasingly expressed a desire to play a more prominent role in guiding the new international students. The students felt that student-to-student interaction and exchange had a special ring of authenticity and relevance. The students argued that they would be seen as credible sources of information to the new international students because of their campus and community experiences. Moreover, the UCLA students also wanted to assume leadership roles in the international student transition process called the International Student and Scholars Orientation Program (ISSOP).

In 1996, Elaine Marchant, then Director of Programs of the ISC discovered The Social Change Model of Leadership Development (SCM) (Higher Education Research Institute [HERI], 1996). As she studied the SCM, she paid special attention to the applicability of the Seven Cs to the creation of the new ISSOP leadership model that she was developing. That year, she decided to enhance the development of the student leaders by partially incorporating the SCM into the training and group process aspects of the program.

In the ensuing years, the former and current Directors of Programs at ISC have altered and improved their approach to student leadership development by integrating experience, practice, research, and trial and error. Throughout this process of continuous improvement, their goals were to create a structure that is fluid in nature to ensure that the project adapts to the specific group of Project Director (PD) interns involved each year. The new PD leadership model therefore incorporates the knowledge and experiences of the Directors of Programs, along with the changing needs of the students, in a model that continues to evolve through time.

The remainder of this chapter examines the most recent leadership development model for ISSOP Project Directors implemented in 1999–2000 by the current Director of Programs and the Orientation Coordinator.

THE 1999 PROJECT DIRECTOR LEADERSHIP MODEL

Through five years of experience working with Project Director student leaders, ISC staff members have agreed that to be effective leaders, Project Directors must be genuinely interested in helping others and respectful of people of different cultures and backgrounds. The Project Directors are extremely important because they have a major impact in the lives of hundreds of new international students and student volunteers. ISC staff members want everyone involved (from the ISC staff themselves and the Project Directors to the participants) to learn from ISSOP. Consequently, they ask that Project Directors lead by example and become role models to the volunteers with whom they work. The premise is that the student leaders can influence and set the tone for the entire Orientation program by acting as role models and promoting a group-leadership approach. For example, if Project Directors are sensitive to the needs of their volunteers and those of the international students, volunteers will be more likely to do the same when working with the new international students. The role of the Project Director is also to "facilitate." They are asked to draw from their volunteers' skills and experiences and to involve them in the process of planning activities for their project groups.

To facilitate the leadership development of the Project Directors that follow the above described non-hierarchical approach, nine principles serve as the foundation of the training for PDs.

Non-Hierarchical Team Work

To build the deepest level of comfort and trust, an ISC staff member announces to the Project Directors our Rule Number One at the beginning of the Project Director Leadership Training. Rule Number One permeates all aspects of the training and is vital to the successful implementation of several elements:

There are no ranks or levels of authority. To get a better understanding of who we are, we ask that you be as honest and open as possible. This will help us get a head start in learning about each other. But please remember that no one is asked to share more than he or she is comfortable sharing. Be considerate of each other and do not judge, interrupt, or finish each other's sentences.

This rule supports the concepts of Congruence, Consciousness of Self, and Group Processes found in the SCM. The rule assumes that the Project Directors will be authentic and will bring candor to the discussion. It also highlights the importance of an individual awareness of personal values. Rule One sets the stage for all other training elements.

Self-Assessment and Goal Definition

The first step in becoming an effective leader is to understand how we view ourselves or have a consciousness of self. During the first part of the ISSOP Leadership Training, the Project Director team members are asked to participate in an introspection exercise in which they identify their own strengths, motivations, and areas for improvement. In addition, they are asked to establish personal goals to be achieved by the end of their internship and to share this information with their team members. After listening to the self-assessment of Project Director interns, ISC staff members debrief the exercise by pointing out to the team that the strengths of each Project Director are varied. ISC staff facilitators proceed by encouraging Project Directors to make note of each other's skills and to consult those who possess the skills they desire to strengthen. Through such collaborative efforts, the team learns that their combined talents form a sum greater than the whole. Not only do the Project Directors grow as individuals, but they also come to understand their unique contributions, the unique contributions of others, and the powerful dynamic that is created by truly working together.

Sharing a Common Goal

Once ISC staff members identify the individual goals of the Project Directors, they ask Project Directors about what motivated them to become involved as leaders for ISSOP. The ISC staff helps the Project Directors identify and agree upon a common goal, which revolves around effective Orientation services to international students. The identification of a common goal is consistent with the principle of Common Purpose as defined in the SCM.

Once the goals of the Project Directors as a team have been defined, the ISC staff describe the roles each individual Project Director will play in bringing about the identified group goals. By this point, Project Directors have established a commitment to work towards achieving their personal goals and have demonstrated a commitment to their team members. The third principle is also designed to promote commitment to the mission of ISC, which is to facilitate the development of cross-cultural understanding.

Work Ethics and Styles

To take advantage of the opportunities group work can provide, the Project Directors spend time learning about their own and their team members' work-styles. To make progress on reaching effective collaborative relationships, Project Directors and ISC staff participate in a facilitated discussion about previous work experiences. Each describes their first work experience and talks about what they learned from it. Project Directors and ISC staff also share what they have learned about work through their families. By bringing to the forefront important experiences and role models, this exercise helps the team to understand each member's working culture. In the final portion of this exercise, the particular working styles of the ISC staff and the Project Directors are discussed. At this point, Project Directors can identify work skills that other Project Directors have and how they may benefit from working as a group. They leave with a better understanding of the group's working culture and a sense of the importance of collaboration.

Communication

Communication is the most important area to explore in working with people from different cultures. It is extremely important to understand that cultures and individuals communicate differently. Although it would be impossible to learn every way of communicating (since there are as many communication styles as there are people in this world), it is very useful to learn about as many types of communication as possible. This information becomes a useful tool when working with students from different cultures and backgrounds. For example, direct and indirect communication vary between people of different cultural

backgrounds. The common Orientation goal of facilitating cross-cultural understanding attempts to address this variance.

In working with ISSOP staff, project directors, students, and volunteers, ISC
staff has found that most of the obstacles encountered by those involved with
ISSOP can be attributed to miscommunication and lack of understanding of the
people's varied cultures. It is therefore important that volunteers, staff, and Project Directors practice active listening with each other and the international students they serve. This is done by paying attention to verbal (e.g., word choices
and intonation) as well as non-verbal (e.g., body language, gestures, physical
expressions) communication. During training, Project Directors participate in
various exercises that highlight various modes of communication.

Culture

Culture is broadly defined in this chapter as the views and behaviors that
result from a person's belonging to many varied sub-cultures. For example, a
particular individual may be of Mexican heritage and carry that cultural element
with her. This will affect the way she perceives her life and many of her experiences. This same person may also be bisexual. Her experiences as a Mexican
woman will be therefore altered by her being bisexual and differ from those of
another Mexican woman who is not. By defining culture as the sum of many
important sub-cultures, one can begin to understand the complexities involved
when interacting with different people. In the same way that cultures and sub-
cultures affect a person's view, the values and belief systems of individuals may
differ between people of the same culture(s). (See the third section of this volume for a broader discussion of the complex relationship between leadership
and identity.)

One of the most challenging and enriching aspects for ISC staff and volunteers working with international students from 130 countries is gaining exposure
to a great variety of cultures. Contrary to what some people may still believe,
culture is not limited to the political borders of a nation. When discussing culture, ISC staff members ask Project Directors and volunteers to think about their
own cultures and how they differ from those of their parents and neighbors. The
importance of understanding one's culture is also stressed in the SCM, through
the value, Consciousness of Self.

In addition to being able to span national boundaries, culture is fluid. When
we compare our own personal culture of ten years ago with that of today, we
might learn that some of our views have changed because of an experience or
a conversation we had with someone with whom we might have initially disa-
greed, but who altered our views. One example of how this concept is developed
during Project Director training is an exercise in which the student leaders are
asked to share a life-changing experience with the group and talk about how
that experience has affected who they are.

ISSOP staff understand that culture is rich and complex and that understanding their own cultures and being open-minded and non-judgmental will help them in facilitating Orientation and in growing personally and professionally. During training, Project Directors are asked to think of their own culture, explore the various cultures they belong to, and think of how these affect their views of life and the way they relate to others. They do this in part by creating a "Cultural Self-Portrait" and presenting it to the group. Sharing and talking about the cultures of the Project Directors teaches them and ISC staff a great deal about diversity and motivations to interact a certain way. It also prepares Project Directors for the diversity they will encounter when dealing with volunteers and new international students during the Orientation program.

Context

After discussing and exploring goals, cultural elements, and diversity, it is important to make the link between who we are and where we work. During a portion of the Project Director training, the Director of the ISC provides an explanation of the organization's culture by providing a historical background and sharing the ISC mission. In discussing the mission, the Director of ISC explores a greater circle: the context of Orientation, and within that, Project Directors, volunteers, and staff find their respective roles. The larger context for ISC and ISSOP participants is the city of Los Angeles, a multicultural city that is constantly changing. The contextual goal therefore becomes to create the link between UCLA and Los Angeles to help the new international students understand the nature of the community in which they will live. Project Directors are encouraged to explore this community and think of ways in which their particular volunteers could assist the international students in gaining a better understanding of their new environment in order to have a richer experience during their stay at UCLA.

The Power of Diversity

The richness of diversity at UCLA is astonishing. UCLA has approximately 7,500 international students from 130 different countries (5,500 immigrants and 2,000 non-immigrants) and 1,700 international scholars. In addition, the ethnic, religious, cultural, and social viewpoints that are found among the over 33,000 UCLA students cross many boundaries. ISC staff members encourage Project Directors to learn from the diverse volunteers and the students who participate in the International Students and Scholars Orientation Program. In the initial phases of the training, Project Directors discuss the fact that most people carry stereotypes from which they draw, even unintentionally. This point is underscored by having the Project Directors play the *IA (International Advisor) Detective* game in which the student leaders are paired up and asked to silently "write down what they see." In debriefing, the *IA Detective* brings attention to the reality that as we meet new people, some of us have the tendency to use stereotypes to interpret and evaluate people's behaviors and appearances. These stereotypes result from what we have learned through the various cultures and experiences that we bring with us. ISC staff advises Project Directors to be aware of the danger that this may happen, so that they can avoid making erroneous interpretations or evaluations when they meet new international students.

The Project Directors and volunteers are urged to step away from those stereotypes by keeping an open and non-judgmental mind. Project Directors are encouraged to learn from their differences and to draw from the knowledge and different perspectives that people bring to the table. To help illustrate the important contributions of a diverse group, Project Directors and volunteers participate in a game called *Just us!*, created by Ashay, a non-profit organization based in Los Angeles. During *Just us!* Project Directors are divided into two small groups and asked to come up with as many answers as possible for one given question (e.g., how to say thank you in different languages). The purpose of this game is to help participants reach the conclusion that the more diverse the group, the richer it is. The broader interpretation of this exercise is that when faced with a problem, a group that is diverse will be able to come up with a greater number of solutions to the same problem than a homogenous group. The job of the leaders is to bring these skills to the table by encouraging volunteers to voice their opinions and be open to solving problems with an approach that may be different from their traditional way of solving them.

Trust and the Team

To build a sense of team, Project Directors work together in many areas beginning with training and continuing through the Orientation program itself. At the beginning of their leadership training, Project Directors participate in exercises, such as the *Trust Walk* to develop open communication and trust. Building trust is important because as team members, Project Directors rely on one another for the entirety of the program's success. At the end of these exercises, ISSOP staff stress the importance of clear communication and direction by the leader for building the trust of his or her team members. In addition, Project Directors discover that when a person accepts the power to lead a group towards a particular goal, he or she also acquires a great amount of responsibility to his or her team members.

CONCLUSION

While not a perfect model, the model described above for implementing non-hierarchical leadership best meets our diverse campus's need to empower international students as newcomers, leaders, and volunteers. A key strength of our model is that, in addition to being conscious of the new international students' needs, it is also respectful of the varied cultures and backgrounds of the people involved in the complex process of assisting international students to adjust to UCLA and Los Angeles.

I recognize that the search for an ideal model of student leadership development is by no means over. On the contrary, just as we encourage students to continue growing, I believe that to improve the Center's programs, ISC staff must remain current with our constituents' changing needs by continuously evaluating and revising programs. After all, this is a changing world and flexibility and adaptability is what will keep us up to date.

The Center's most valuable critics will always remain the students involved in its programs. However, ISC staff have found that the research and study of other university programs, as well as collaboration with university departments, have been extremely useful in helping reach an effective model of leadership development for this organization. I therefore welcome feedback from other institutions and at the same time encourage others to learn from the various student leadership development programs that exist throughout the United States and the world.

REFERENCE

Higher Education Research Institute. (1996). *A Social Change Model of Leadership Development* (3rd ed.). Los Angeles: Author.

Section III

The Complex Intersections of Leadership and Identity

REFLECTIONS FROM UCLA STUDENTS

In my experience with the Bruin Leaders Project, I learned the significance of diversity in leadership. Diversity provides everyone with numerous voices to listen to and take into consideration when making decisions and forming opinions. I learned this both in theory and in practice. I always felt that my voice was listened to and taken seriously. As a woman, this was not always the case in other activities I had been involved in. College is a time when people are learning about themselves and about who they want to be. It is the perfect time for people to open up and diversify their ideas about who can be a leader and what he or she can do in that position. The traditional "male" model of leadership as an individual endeavor still plays an important role, but I have found that a collaborative, more "female" model has found a place in all aspects of working with others. I personally have learned that if I take myself seriously as a leader and as a woman, others have no choice but to do the same.

—Netta Avineri

As a woman involved in Bruin Leaders, I actually felt that I could make a difference and that there are people willing to listen to what I have to say.

—Jennifer Su

Every individual has the ability to positively change society, to become a leader in their home or community by simply bringing hope, a smile, or some words of compassion to another human being. Their leadership is not characterized by their position or standing in the eyes of others, but rather by the process they follow to initiate that change. In this competitive society in which we live, where there are a few "rulers" and many "followers," we must all see the potential to lead in our own unique way. We must all learn the qualities of collaboration and inclusion and put these behaviors into practice in our daily interactions if we want any possibility of resolving the leadership crisis in the United States and expanding the definition of leadership to include those individuals who are unable to see their potential as leaders.

—Joe Manko

Chapter 19

Intercultural Leadership: A Program Model for Students in Higher Education

Daniel C. Adams and Patricia M. Aqui

INTRODUCTION

Given technological advances, demographic shifts, and other sociopolitical and economic changes throughout the world, higher education institutions need to recognize international and domestic imperatives for understanding culture's role in interpersonal and intergroup interactions. Currently college and university graduates enter a complex, dynamic world where economic survival is dependent upon individual and collective abilities to interact successfully with people from various countries (Lustig & Koester, 1993). The emergent presence of students from a wide diversity of racial, ethnic, gender, sexual orientation, age, religious, spiritual, ability, and socio-economic backgrounds on United States higher education campuses (Zuniga, Nagda, Sevig, Thompson, & Dey, 1995) has necessitated an appreciation for domestic cultural diversity. Correspondingly, higher education institutions develop social identity group course requirements, implement recruitment and retention programs for various cultural populations, and advance efforts to create an inclusive institutional climate (Magner, 1990; Schoem, 1991, 1993; Tatum, 1992; Zuniga et al., 1995).

Despite these institutional efforts to encourage intercultural relationships, student interactions (regardless of their U.S. domestic or international status) continue to be fraught with intercultural anxiety (Stephan & Stephan, 1985; Zuniga et al., 1995). International students studying in the United States have some trepidation regarding their social interactions with others. Their concerns generally encompass understanding spoken U.S. English and reciprocally being understood, identifying themselves as international and having multiple cultural identities, developing friendships with U.S. nationals, and understanding U.S. values (Kato, 1999; Marino, 1997). Typically, international students do not participate in co-curricular activities, including those focusing on nationality or ethnicity (Marino, 1997) thereby limiting opportunities for all students to develop intercultural relationships.

In addition, educators and educational institutions must address students' fear and anxiety concerning cultural diversity and intercultural interactions. Students with limited experience interacting in culturally diverse social situations may respond to intellectual, ethical, and social diversity as threatening experiences and resist learning about diversity (Ascher, 1990; Tatum, 1992; Wiener, 1990). Furthermore, students who believe in "the correctness of their worldview" become intimidated by cultural and intellectual multiplicity. Their responses include denying the existence of diversity, refusing to see its validity, attacking it as something evil and "hat[ing] those who believe differently" (Dalton, 1991). Therefore, a compelling challenge and opportunity exists for educators to design student-centered initiatives that alleviate intercultural anxiety and stimulate interest in promoting successful interactions with people of diverse cultures, nationalities and life experiences.

Administrative departments, academic requirements, and programs that enhance cultural plurality alone are insufficient to address anxiety and resistance towards cultural diversity. Co-curricular programs supplement these efforts by providing student-centered, structured, and practical learning to address these barriers outside of the classroom environment. The Intercultural Leadership Seminar (ILS) at the University of Michigan is one such program presenting possibilities for leadership development and improving intercultural interactions inclusive of international and U.S. domestic cultural diversity. This program format synthesizes these two opportunities through a leadership development model founded upon theories from the fields of non-hierarchical leadership, intercultural relations, and communication.

CULTURAL INFLUENCES UPON LEADERSHIP

"Leadership" and "effective leadership" evoke numerous ideas and beliefs for people in the field of leadership education. Fundamental to leadership is an understanding of people, their culture and their institutions (Adler, 1991). Generally, U.S. leadership development programs endeavor to develop effective leaders possessing leadership traits and skills from a particular cultural orientation (Hoppe, 1998). These programs produce competent leaders who operate in an environment with people possessing *similar* cultural orientations. When these same *monoculturally* effective leaders function in an environment with people possessing *divergent* cultural orientations, their monocultural skill set is rendered ineffectual. This result confirms internationally conducted research indicating that well-meaning clashes occur when leaders impose their views regarding the role of leader in a cultural context other than their own (Brislin, 1993). Moreover, when people possessing disparate leadership cultural orientations participate in U.S. leadership programs (for example, someone with an

Ojibway or Kenyan cultural orientation), responses often include puzzlement and dissatisfaction with outcomes (Hoppe, 1998).

Non-hierarchical leadership perspectives offer alternative options for applying leadership skills in diverse cultural contexts. Intercultural leadership is one such perspective that entails including and employing cultural differences that develop common understanding in collaboration with people of diverse cultural backgrounds through culturally appropriate behavior. This leadership standpoint advances the possibility of transcending the confines of one's cultural worldview by developing intercultural competence. Intercultural competence esteems human differences and believes that knowledge, awareness, attitudes, and skills are crucial for an inclusive approach to human diversity. Therefore, interculturally competent leadership requires: (1) an acknowledgment that successful leaders possess the ability to empathize and understand people *on their own terms* (Fantini, 1991); and (2) a lifelong commitment to learn culturally appropriate behaviors. Leadership development programs focused on facilitating intercultural competence can cultivate inclusive leaders with this understanding and commitment.

Assumptions about Culture

Several basic assumptions regarding culture undergird this leadership context. This perspective presumes that culture is constructed, dynamic, and learned through interactions with others rather than an immutable, essentialist set of guidelines to which societies adhere. Hence, we learn about our culture's assumptions about life and appropriate behaviors through socialization with others in our community—family, church, school, and neighborhood. Culture therefore encompasses a *learned set of shared perceptions* including beliefs, values, and norms that influence the behaviors of a relatively large group of people (Lustig & Koester, 1993).

Secondly, culture operates at interpersonal and group interaction levels. Culture frames our identity in a manner that defines not only how we see ourselves, but also how others see us. Thus culture involves aspects of social identity including race, ethnicity, gender, sexual orientation, age, physical and mental abilities, socioeconomic status, and religious affiliation or spirituality. Furthermore, this assumption about culture values the rich confluence of multiple identities (e.g., brother, father, husband, Filipino, Catholic, and golfer) that comprise who we consider ourselves to be.

Lastly, culture permeates everyone's worldview to the extent that we take it for granted (Brislin, 1993) and are unconscious of culture's influence upon how we understand and interpret the phenomena of the world (Fantini, 1991). Consequently, we fail to understand that culture provides us *one of many valid ways* (rather than the *only* way) to perceive, interpret, and evaluate the world and people around us. Awareness of our cultural idiosyncrasies unfortunately heightens during well-meaning clashes with culturally divergent people. Our responses range from misunderstanding to intolerance for different cultural worldviews and behavior. Therefore, alternative cognitive, affective, and behavioral responses become necessary when we encounter cultural differences.

Intercultural Communication

Interactions are intercultural when the degree of cultural differentiation between the people involved is sufficiently large and important that it creates dissimilar interpretations and expectations about what is accepted as competent communication behaviors (Lustig & Koester, 1993). Accordingly, interactions have varying degrees of cultural difference that arise during the communication process. Figure 19.1 illustrates the range of intercultural interactions involving aspects of U.S. cultural diversity (e.g., gender, sexual orientation, class, and so on) *and* international diversity (e.g., interactions with citizens from other countries). While this figure was created with the University of Michigan in mind, the continuum it represents is relevant for other campuses and contexts as well.

This continuum is merely a simplistic scale to provide concrete examples illustrating basic differences between intracultural and intercultural interactions. As with all theoretical models, it is not a precise representation of reality's complexity. The degree to which an interaction is perceived as intracultural or intercultural varies depending upon a number of individual factors such as history, life experience, beliefs, and so on, and from whose standpoint one is judging. However, this framework provides an entry point into acknowledging and understanding the contextual, dynamic complexity of multiple, intersecting cultural identities that people possess during their interactions.

Intercultural Communication Competence

Intercultural communication skills that initiate a dialogue process are imperative to understanding people's cultural framework and how they perceive, interpret, and evaluate their interactions. Although many characterizations of intercultural competence exist, common threads of (1) establishing and maintaining positive relationships, (2) effective communication with minimal loss and distortion, and (3) achievement of appropriate levels of cooperation and collaboration with others (Fantini, 1991) emerge. Table 19.1 specifies appropriate cognitive, affective, and behavioral responses needed for demonstrating intercultural competence during intercultural interactions. More significantly, leaders seeking collaboration in intercultural interactions must demonstrate these competencies that create common understanding among culturally diverse people (Adler, 1991; Dalton, 1998; Kouzes & Posner, 1995; Moran & Riesenberger, 1994).

Figure 19.1
Continuum of Student Intercultural Interactions at the University of Michigan

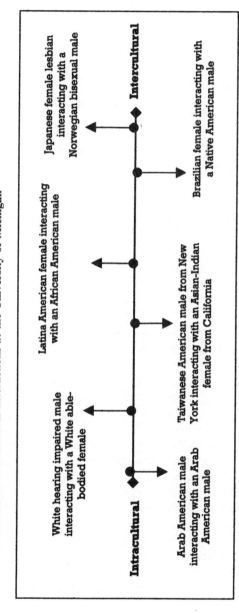

Table 19.1
Behavioral Dimensions of Intercultural Competence

Display of respect	The ability to express respect and positive regard for another
Interaction posture	The ability to respond to others in descriptive, non-evaluative, and non-judgmental ways
Orientation to knowledge	The terms people use to explain themselves and their world
Empathy	The capacity to behave as if you understand the world as others do
Task role behavior	Behaviors that involve the initiation of ideas related to group problem-solving activities
Relational role behavior	Behaviors associated with interpersonal harmony and mediation
Interaction management	Skill in regulating conversations
Tolerance for ambiguity	The ability to react to new and ambiguous situations with little visible discomfort

Source: Lustig & Koester (1993).

Intercultural Leadership

Given the need for leadership competency, intercultural competence is a touchstone for developing intercultural leadership skills. Intercultural leadership competence requires utilizing a repertoire of communication behaviors in a manner appropriate to the demands of the situation-abilities central to developing a common understanding from cultural differences. Intercultural leadership development draws upon several theoretical bases to develop alternative cognitive, affective, and behavioral responses to interacting with cultural differences. The knowledge and awareness bases draw upon intercultural relations and intercultural communication theories. The behavioral base draws upon non-hierarchical leadership and intercultural competence theory. Accordingly, intercultural leadership development prepares emerging leaders for intercultural interactions through raising awareness regarding culture's influence on worldviews, developing an appreciation for the richness of humanity's diversity, decreasing intercultural anxiety, improving intercultural communication skills, and developing interculturally competent behaviors.

INTERCULTURAL LEADERSHIP PROGRAM MODEL

Institutional Support

The University of Michigan's leadership education vision emphasizes programming that "prepares students to serve as contributing members of a multicultural society and an interdependent world" (MLI Taskforce, 1997). This progressive vision offers a fitting framework for an intercultural leadership development program at the University of Michigan. Additionally, the institutional guiding principle of "recogni[zing] and valu[ing] the interconnectedness of curricular and co-curricular arenas" (MLI Taskforce, 1997) presents a context for purposeful programmatic planning. Hence, program development and implementation model collaboration, common understanding, and commitment toward improving intercultural interactions on multiple levels. At one level, past participants contribute a vital component to this student-centered leadership program by serving as peer facilitators in subsequent sessions. A partnership among higher education institutions through the involvement of facilitators (including this chapter's co-authors) from the University of Michigan, University of Minnesota, and Washington State University is another example of collaboration at another level.

Needs Assessment

Prior to the design of the University of Michigan's intercultural leadership program, 105 students who had expressed interest in developing their intercultural leadership skills participated in a needs assessment. In this assessment, students were asked the following open-ended questions: (1) How do you define an intercultural leader; and (2) What knowledge, skills, and attitudes do intercultural leaders possess? The following excerpts from these surveys reveal students' views regarding intercultural leaders and leadership:

> . . . conscious and critically aware of the multiple ways that culture manifests within individuals and social structures.

> . . . aware of the limits of their own direct understanding . . . have empathy, imagination, and motivation to try to understand beyond what they directly cannot know.

> . . . must not be just a *good listener* but one who strives to hear with all available senses, the heart, and intuition.

> . . . knows that understanding is not merely a cognitive or intellectual process, but a process that requires our attention on all levels.

> . . . is self-reflective, self-aware, and willing to question and suspend their assumptions, beliefs, and personal dramas of how the world and other people should be.

Qualitative data analysis suggests that the competencies students articulated corroborate with Lustig and Koester's (1993) intercultural competence behavioral dimensions. Eighty-three respondents stated that both verbal and non-verbal communication skills are essential for an intercultural leader, particularly active listening skills. These data appear to confirm the need for an intercultural leadership programming approach that facilitates interpersonal skill development, develops an intercultural knowledge base, and increases affective capacities for interacting with cultural differences (Dalton, 1999).

Marketing and Recruitment

Program marketing targets international student groups, U.S. cultural diversity groups, and mainstream student groups equally to ensure a wide range of culturally diverse participants. Students complete a program application as an assessment of their readiness to learn about others within the context of intercultural leadership. Ideal applicants include undergraduate and graduate students seeking personal and professional knowledge, attitudes, and skills development regarding intercultural relations at interpersonal and intergroup levels. No more than 40 students participate to allow for equitable contribution in small and large group discussions. Hence, participants have the unique opportunity to engage in intensive dialogue with others who share a commitment to strengthening their own intercultural competence.

Program Development and Design

The Intercultural Leadership Seminar (ILS) is a four-day leadership development program designed to provide participants with a deeper understanding of how to interact more effectively in intercultural settings. The curriculum content is based upon data collected from the student needs assessment and theories related to intercultural relations, leadership, and communication. The goals for the seminar fall under the categories of cultural knowledge, inclusive attitudes, and leadership skills associated with developing intercultural competence. Because direct experiences and experiential approaches are appropriate methods for developing all of these capacities (Fantini, 1991), the program design utilizes structured small and large group discussions, simulations, and group exercises. Additionally, the design is sequenced developmentally from interpersonal to intergroup to intercultural levels. Sequencing in this manner offers participants the opportunity to transcend the limitations of their worldview by provoking an examination of their identity, perspectives, and culture in relation to others.

A *cultural knowledge* base is crucial to reflecting upon and understanding culture's influence on one's worldviews and everyday interactions, principally regarding leadership and leadership behavior. This base is essential for identifying cultural differences and universal similarities in U.S. and international contexts. To create this knowledge foundation, participants share a component of their culture with the group and engage in large and small group discussions sharing experiences with cultural differences. Activities that expand the participant knowledge base include simulations such as *Barnga* (a simulation that allows participants to experience subtle differences in culture and to practice understanding and reconciling differences to function more effectively in cross-cultural groups) and *Four Corners* (an activity that helps participants to develop a cultural group profile and provide a foundation for examining multiple privileges and oppression).

Strengthening participant appreciation and respect for the richness of cultural diversity is the focus of developing an *inclusive attitude* base. Within this arena, participants are encouraged to explore and examine the roots of their own and other's intercultural anxiety. To reduce intercultural anxiety, participants learn to identify their "hot buttons" and examine their responses to well-meaning cultural clashes and acts of bias. Viewing and discussing videos such as *The Color of Fear* (Wah, 1994) is one way to address intercultural anxiety. Foundational activities that develop inclusive attitudes help participants understand the validity of other cultural frameworks and understand the historical, political, and economic basis of current inequalities. More importantly, an inclusive attitude provides the basis for a person to make informed and deliberate decisions on appropriate behavior in intercultural contexts that foster collaboration and positive interactions. *The Tower Project* (a team activity that explores issues of multicultural team building and cooperative learning) is one such activity that develops this lifelong commitment to learning interculturally competent behavior. This particular simulation fosters the need for inclusion by surfacing issues related to marginality, in-group/out-group dynamics, multiple perspectives, power, privilege, coalition-building, and intergroup conflict.

Intercultural leadership skills are the tangible expression and product of intercultural knowledge and awareness. Throughout the program, participants are encouraged to develop intercultural communication skills, particularly active listening skills. Out of listening and engaging in dialogue, participants learn to explore different perspectives on the concepts of teamwork and leadership. Consequently, participants develop different ways to create intercultural teams and develop a peer coalition committed to creating positive change on campus. Participants learn the indispensable leadership skill set of managing intercultural conflict.

Program Evaluation and Outcomes

Participant responses to the seminar reflect paradigm shifts regarding intercultural interactions. All the participants state that they would recommend the program to others, which is an important result for recruiting future participants. An overwhelming majority (97%) considered the program valuable and useful to them in future leadership positions. The following statements from program evaluations articulate the transformative power of students' experiences with the program.

I feel more confident and relaxed with people of different cultures now because of the diverse viewpoints I encountered at ILS. What surprised me the most wasn't what I learned about other cultures but what I learned about myself. You can't understand the world until you understand yourself.

Especially after a few specific conversations, I was really interested to discover the difference in what Americans thought it meant to be American, and what people looking in at our culture thought it meant to be American.

As a newcomer to this country, I had plenty of questions around sensitive issues. ILS taught me how easy it can be to communicate with people from other cultures without being offensive. The most important thing I learned from ILS was that although people come from different backgrounds, we all have the ability to meet on common ground.

Positive outcomes that result from program participation exist on several levels. Some student participants develop self-confidence and go on to become student leaders in campus organizations or become resident hall advisors. Other students go on to participate in national internships such as the Congressional Black Caucus and other programs outside the university system such as the Chinese Synergy Program for Outstanding Youth. Faculty facilitators report benefits from collaboration in the program as well. Student and faculty facilitators engender a strong sense of community and establish personal relationships that foster mutual learning.

A major factor of the model's success lies in the participants' tendency to be open to learning about themselves and others. International and U.S. students report that they developed a more global viewpoint on many issues simply by listening to each other's perspectives. Moreover, these conversations result in a greater awareness and understanding of international student needs and experiences at the University of Michigan. Furthermore, the seminar experience encourages ideas and initiatives that bridge cultural chasms on campus, particularly between international and U.S. students. The following remark made by an ILS participant from Iran reflects the global scope of promoting cultural understanding: "I hope we all take our invaluable lessons of peace and friendship and spread them across continents. We need to be ambassadors for these kinds of programs."

CONCLUSION

Before the early 1980s, few administrators in higher education could have predicted the globalization of U.S. society and the ramifications of adapting to globalization. As leadership programming continues to become a priority for many U.S. institutions of higher learning, student affairs professionals must consider programs that examine leadership from an intercultural perspective. Intercultural leadership development is crucial to preparing students to meet the ever-changing demands of a global society. Given the phenomenon of cultural pluralism across higher education campuses nationally, this program model can be adapted easily to the leadership development needs of students.

Interculturally competent leadership recognizes multiple approaches to developing effective leaders according to cultural context. Traditional approaches have value and are effective within particular U.S. intracultural contexts. This leadership model offers another framework for developing competent leadership behaviors within a continuum of intracultural *and* intercultural contexts. Effective leaders within these varying cultural contexts must use the full repertoire of leadership behaviors available to them and deliberately select styles more appropriate to the unique demands of the situation (Lipman-Blumen, 1996). Most importantly, this model uses all of the resources available to create common understanding and collaboration among a culturally diverse group of people.

Although we promote intercultural contact actively and the positive value of cultural diversity, not everyone shares this perspective. For some, cultural pluralism is a perplexing phenomenon that evokes ambivalent feelings of "hope and concern . . . optimism and pessimism about the prospects for social life among peoples from differing racial and cultural groups" (Duster, 1991). More specifically, some display resistance and discomfort with embracing cultural diversity. Others fear that the inclusion of cultural diversity presents too many complex ethical dilemmas in which people forsake their morals and principles for "cultural relativity." However, we believe cultural plurality cultivates commitment to our worldviews by stimulating an examination of our culture, ethics, and actions. Cultural diversity helps us explore and develop alternative perspectives that we never consider because our cultural frameworks limit available options.

Primarily, we are convinced that cultural plurality is enriching. The most rewarding aspect for us as facilitators is what the students *teach us* from the time of their application to the end of the program session. During these sessions, we bear witness to the transformative power of positive human relations. We appreciate this rare opportunity to spend concentrated time listening to student voices as they engage in critical, poignant dialogues regarding their own and others' experiences with cultural diversity. We marvel at their insightful ideas about global citizenship and their courage in making commitments to be more inclusive human beings. Above all, we find renewal and community from discovering kindred spirits who revere the richness and unlimited potential of humanity.

REFERENCES

Adler, N.J. (1991). *International dimensions of organizational behavior.* Boston: PWS-Kent.

Ascher, C. (1990). Ensuring a rainbow after the storm: Recent initiatives to institutionalize pluralism on predominantly white campuses. *Higher Education Extension Review, 2*(1).

Brislin, R. (1993). *Culture's influence on behavior.* Orlando, FL: Holt, Rinehart and Winston.

Dalton, J. C. (1991). Racial and ethnic backlash in college peer culture. *New Directions for Student Services, 56,* 3–12.

Dalton, J. C. (1999). *Beyond borders: How international developments are changing the student affairs practice.* San Francisco: Jossey-Bass.

Dalton, M. (1998). Developing leaders for global roles. In C.D. McCauley, R. S. Moxley, & E. Van Velsor (Eds.), *The center for creative leadership handbook of leadership development* (pp. 379–402). San Francisco: Jossey-Bass.

Duster, T. (1991, September 25). Understanding self-segregation on the campus. *Chronicle of Higher Education,* B1.

Fantini, A. (1991, February). Becoming better global citizens: The promise of intercultural competence. *Adult Learning, 2,* 15–19.

Hoppe, M. (1998). Cross-cultural issues in leadership development. In C. D. McCauley, R. S. Moxley, & E. Van Velsor (Eds.), *The center for creative leadership handbook of leadership development.* San Francisco: Jossey-Bass.

Kato, N. (1999, Fall/Winter). Working with gay, lesbian and bisexual international students in the United States. *International Educator,* 29–34.

Kouzes, J. M., & Posner, B. Z. (1995). *The leadership challenge.* San Francisco: Jossey-Bass.

Lipman-Blumen, J. (1996). *The connective edge: Leading in an interdependent world.* San Francisco: Jossey-Bass.

Lustig, M., & Koester, J. (1993). *Intercultural competence: Interpersonal communication across cultures.* New York: HarperCollins College Publishers.

Magner, D. (1990, March 28). Difficult questions in courses that explore race issues. *Chronicle of Higher Education,* A19.

Marino, T. (1997). What bothers international students? *NAFSA: Association of International Educators Newsletter, 48*(6), 1, 22–23.

Michigan Leadership Initiatives Taskforce (MLI). (1997). *Vision for leadership education at the University of Michigan.* Appendix B. Ann Arbor: University of Michigan.

Moran, R. T., & Riesenberger, J. R. (1994). *The global challenge: Building the new world enterprise.* London: McGraw-Hill.

Schoem, D. (1991, April 3). College students need thoughtful and in-depth study of race relations. *Chronicle of Higher Education,* A48.

Schoem, D. (1993). Teaching about ethnic identity and intergroup relations. In D. Schoem, L. Frankel, X. Zuniga, & E. Lewis (Eds.), *Multicultural teaching in the university.* Westport, CT: Praeger.

Stephan W. G. & Stephan, C. W. (1985). Intergroup anxiety. *Journal of Social Issues, 41,* 157–166.

Tatum, B. D. (1992). Talking about race, learning about racism: The application of racial identity development theory in the classroom. *Harvard Educational Review, 62*(1), 1–24.

Wah, L. M. (1994). *The Color of Fear.* 90 min. Berkeley, CA: Stir-Fry Productions. Videocassette.

Wiener, J. (1990, February 26). Words that wound: Free speech for campus bigots? *The Nation.*

1994). More recently, an assessment of student involvement in leadership development programs indicated empirical evidence of student growth in civic responsibility, leadership skills, multicultural awareness, and understanding of personal values (Astin & Cress, 1998). Further, a comparison of institutions with and without leadership programs indicated that even students who attend schools with leadership programs, but who *do not* participate in such programs, show greater increases in self-assessment of leadership ability and civic responsibility than students at colleges and universities without leadership programs on campus (Astin & Cress, 1998). In other words, there is something about the culture of these institutions that communicates uniquely to students the importance of leadership development and citizenship. If we create cultures of participatory assessment and leadership on our college campuses, then societal change is sure to follow.

CONCLUSION

Over two decades ago, Bowen (1977) commented that "most of the leaders in our society in virtually all walks of life are college educated, and it may be presumed that the cognitive and affective traits developed or strengthened in college would be useful to them; yet it is apparently not known whether higher education helps people to combine these traits in ways that produce the quality we call leadership" (p. 142). While some studies have assessed the role of higher education in developing citizen leaders (Astin & Cress, 1998; Moriarty, 1994), more work has yet to be done.

A myriad of resources exist that provide specific strategies for actually performing quantitative and quality assessment (Angelo, 1998; Banta, Lund, Black, & Oblander, 1996; Cress, 1996; Driscoll et al., 1998; Erwin, 1991; Jacobs & Chase, 1992; Kezar, 1998; McMillan, 1988; Middaugh, Trusheim, & Bauer, 1994; Miller, 1979; Schuh & Upcraft, 1998; Tyree, 1998). The focus of this chapter was to present a philosophical framework for thinking about how and why to engage in participatory assessment. Along these same lines, Tierney (1993) emphasizes that we must develop assessment as a formative activity and create assessment as an on-going process that involves the entire community. Heywood (1989), in fact, suggests that assessment is more than just a way of thinking about or doing education, "it is a way of life."

Of course, in any group process there is always the danger of "group-think," which can exclude individuals and different ideas (Bensimon & Neumann, 1993). Also, faculty and staff may resist attempts to change procedures that they consider their sole purview. In addition, students may not feel they have the skills or qualifications to judge their own or others work and/or feel that they are paying the institution to provide them such assessment and feedback.

If, however, we return to the fundamental principles of the Social Change Model (trust, openness, honesty, inclusiveness, and communication), we can create conditions by which disagreement is respected and where alternative ideas fuel the creative process. We must not shy away from assessment but rather embrace the participatory concepts and integrate them into our learning and leadership development efforts. Ultimately, our use of the participatory model of learning and assessment is sure to assist in achieving our goals for higher education in developing sound academic minds, empathetic leaders, and caring citizens.

REFERENCES

Angelo, T. A. (Ed). (1998). Classroom assessment and research: An update on uses, approaches, and research findings. *New directions for teaching and learning*. San Francisco: Jossey-Bass.

Angelo, T. A. (1999). Doing assessment as if learning matters most. *AAHE Bulletin*, 3–6.

Astin, A. W. (1991a). *Assessment for excellence: The philosophy and practice of assessment and evaluation in higher education*. Washington, DC: American Council on Education.

Astin, A. W. (1991b). Campus life and the college environment. In P. Van Dyke (Ed.), *Keeping the promise: Achieving and maintaining quality in undergraduate education* (pp. 1–11). Washington, DC: American Association of State Colleges and Universities.

Astin, A. W. (1999). Assessment, student development, and public policy. In S. J. Messick (Ed.), *Assessment in higher education* (pp. 157–175). Mahwah, NJ: Lawrence Erlbaum Associates.

Astin, H. S., & Cress, C. M. (1998). *The impact of leadership programs on student development. Technical Report to the W. K. Kellogg Foundation*. Los Angeles: Higher Education Research Institute, University of California.

Astin, H. S., & Leland, C. (1991). *Women of influence, women of vision: A cross-generational study of leaders and social change*. San Francisco: Jossey-Bass.

Banta, T. W., Lund, J. P., Black, K. E., & Oblander, F. W. (1996). *Assessment in practice: Putting principles to work on college campuses*. San Francisco: Jossey-Bass.

Bensimon, E. M., & Neumann, A. (1993). *Redesigning collegiate leadership: Teams and teamwork in higher education*. Baltimore: Johns Hopkins University Press.

Brown, S., & Knight, P. (1994). *Assessing learners in higher education*. Philadelphia: Kogan Page.

Boud, D. (1995). Assessment and learning: Contradictory or complementary? In P. Knight (Ed.), *Assessment for learning in higher education* (pp. 35–48). London: Kogan Page.

Bowen, H. R. (1977). *Investment in learning*. San Francisco: Jossey-Bass.

Chambers, T. (1992). The development of criteria to evaluate college student leadership programs: A Delphi approach. *Journal of College Student Development, 33*(4), 339–347.

Chickering, A. W. (1999). Personal qualities and human development in higher education: Assessment in the service of educational goals. In S. J. Messick (Ed.), *Assessment in higher education* (pp. 13–33). Mahwah, NJ: Lawrence Erlbaum Associates.

Clark, K. E. (1985). Teaching undergraduates to be leaders. *AAHE Bulletin, 37*(7), 11–14.

Courts, P. L., & McInerney, K. H. (1993). *Assessment in higher education: Politics, pedagogy, and portfolios.* Westport, CT: Praeger.

Cress, C. M. (1996). ERIC review: Measuring success through assessment and testing. *Community College Review, 24*(1), 39–51.

Cross, K. P. (1998). Why learning communities? Why now? *About Campus, 3*(3), 4–11.

Driscoll, A., Gelmon, S. B., Holland, B. A., Kerrigan, S., Spring, A., Grosvold, K., & Longley, M. J. (1998). *Assessing the impact of service learning: A workbook of strategies and methods.* Portland, OR: Center for Academic Excellence, Portland State University.

Erwin, T. D. (1991). *Assessing student learning and development: A guide to the principles, goals and methods of determining college outcomes.* San Francisco: Jossey-Bass.

Ewell, P. T. (1999). Assessment of higher education quality: Promise and politics. In S. J. Messick (Ed.), *Assessment in higher education* (pp. 147–156). Mahwah, NJ: Lawrence Erlbaum Associates.

Farr, B. P., & Trumbull, E. (1997). *Assessment alternatives for diverse classrooms.* Norwood, MA: Christopher-Gordon Publishers.

Giroux, H. (1993). Foreword. In W. G. Tierney, *Building communities of difference: Higher education in the twenty-first century* (pp. ix–xii). Westport, CT: Bergin & Garvey.

Heywood, J. (1989). *Assessment in higher education* (2nd ed.). New York: John Wiley & Sons.

Higher Education Research Institute. (1996). *A Social Change Model of Leadership Development* (3rd ed.). Los Angeles: Author.

Howe, W. (1996). Leadership education: A look across the courses. In F. H. Freeman, K. B. Knott, & M. K. Schwartz (Eds.), *Leadership education 1996–1997: A source book. Vol. 1: Courses and programs* (6th ed., pp. 279–290). Greensboro, NC: Center for Creative Leadership.

Huey, J. (1994, February 21). The leadership industry. *Fortune, 129*(4), 54–56.

Jacobs, L. C., & Chase, C. I. (1992). *Developing and using tests effectively: A guide for faculty.* San Francisco: Jossey-Bass.

Kendrick, J. R. (1996). Outcomes of service-learning in an introduction to sociology course. *Michigan Journal of Community Service Learning, 3*, 72–81.

Kezar, A. J. (1998). Assessing learning outcomes. *About Campus, 3*(4), 28–29.

Knight, M. E., Lumsen, D. L., & Gallaro, D. (1991). *Outcomes assessment at Kean College of New Jersey.* New York: University Press of America.

Laanan, F. S., & Yamasaki, E. (1995). *When the shoe doesn't fit: Developing an alternative to the traditional leadership paradigm.* Paper presented at the Annual Meeting of the Association for the Study of Higher Education, Tucson, AZ.

Liu, G. (1995). Knowledge, foundations, and discourse: Philosophical support for service learning. *Michigan Journal of Community Service Learning, 2*, 5–18.

Markus, G. B., Howard, J. P., & King, D. C. (1993). Integrating community service and classroom instruction enhances learning: Results of an experiment. *Educational Evaluation and Policy Analysis, 15*(4), 410–419.

McMillan, J. H. (Ed.). (1988). *Assessing students' learning.* San Francisco: Jossey-Bass.

McMillan, V. K. (1994). Assessment from the state perspective. In T. H. Bers & M. L. Mittler (Eds.), *Assessment and testing: Myths and realities* (pp. 5–11). San Francisco: Jossey-Bass.

Messick, S. (1999). Technology and the future of higher education assessment. In S. J. Messick (Ed.), *Assessment in higher education* (pp. 245–253). Mahwah, NJ: Lawrence Erlbaum Associates.

Middaugh, M. F., Trusheim, D. W., & Bauer, K. W. (1994). *Strategies for the practice of institutional research: Concepts, resources and applications.* Tallahassee, FL: Association for Institutional Research and North East Association for Institutional Research.

Miller, R. I. (1979). *The assessment of college performance.* San Francisco: Jossey-Bass.

Moriarty, D. M. (1994). *Leadership and the college experience: Changes in undergraduates' perceptions of their leadership ability.* Unpublished doctoral dissertation, University of California, Los Angeles.

National Center for Education Statistics. (1994). *The national assessment of college student learning: Identification of the skills to be taught, learned and assessed.* Report No. NCES 94-286. Washington, DC: U.S. Department of Education, Office of Educational Research and Improvement.

Posner, B. Z., & Brodsky, B. (1992). A leadership development instrument for college students. *Journal of College Student Development, 33*(3), 231–237.

Roberts, D. C. (1981). *Student leadership programs in higher education.* Washington, DC: The American College Personnel Association (ACPA) Publishing Board.

Roberts, D. C. (1997). The changing look of leadership programs. *Concepts & Connections: A Newsletter for Leadership Educators, 5*(2), 1, 3, 4, 11–14.

Ryan, L. (1994). The case for national student leadership on community college issues. *Leadership Abstracts, 7*(6).

Sax, L. J., Astin, A. W., Arredondo, M., & Korn, W. S. (1996). *The American college teacher: National norms for the 1995–96 HERI faculty survey.* Los Angeles: Higher Education Research Institute, UCLA.

Sax, L. J., Astin, A. W., & Astin, H. S. (1996). What were the LSAHE impacts on student volunteers? In *Evaluation of Learn and Serve America, Higher Education: First Year Report.* Santa Monica, CA: RAND Corporation.

Sax, L. J., Astin, A. W., Korn, W. S., & Mahoney, K. M. (1998). *American Freshman National Norms, Fall 1998.* Los Angeles: Higher Education Research Institute, UCLA.

Schuh, J. H., & Upcraft, M. L. (1998). Facts and myths about assessment in student affairs. *About Campus, 3*(5), 2–8.

Schwartz, M. K., Axtman, K. M., & Freeman, F.H. (1998). *The leadership education source book* (7th ed.). Greensboro, NC: Center for Creative Leadership.

Seitz, S., & Pepitone, S. (1996). Servant leadership: A model for developing college students. *Metropolitan Universities: An International Forum, 6*(4), 113–122.

Spitzberg, I. J. (1986). *Introduction to campus programs on leadership.* Report to the Council for Liberal Learning, Association of American Colleges, Washington, DC.

Tierney, W. G. (1993). *Building communities of difference: Higher education in the twenty-first century.* Westport, CT: Bergin & Garvey.

Tyree, T. M. (1998). *Designing an instrument to measure socially responsible leadership using the Social Change Model of Leadership Development.* Unpublished doctoral dissertation, University of Maryland, College Park.

Walker, C., & Angelo, T. (1998). A collective effort classroom assessment technique: Promoting high performance in student teams. In T. Angelo (Ed.), *Classroom assessment and research: An update on uses, approaches, and research findings* (pp. 101–112). San Francisco: Jossey-Bass.

Wechsler, A., & Fogel, J. (1995). The outcomes of a service-learning program. *NSEE Quarterly, 20,* 6–7, 25–26.

Chapter 23

Assessing Non-Hierarchical Leadership

Tracy M. Tyree

What are the leadership needs of our students? What type of leadership programs should we develop? What do our students want and need for leadership development? Who are our services reaching? What kind of impact are we having? These are just a few of the many questions leadership educators may be asking about their students, their programs, and their services. Frequently, we lack adequate information to make effective decisions. Assessment provides this missing link in the decision-making process. It also serves to guide practice, identify needs and outcomes, increase effectiveness, inform action, enhance decision making, evaluate and improve programs, and form policies and procedures (Erwin, 1993, 1996; Patrick & Niles, 1988; Patton, 1990).

As Cress indicates in Chapter 22 of this volume, assessment is playing a more critical role than ever in higher education. Competing demands for fiscal resources, shortages in human resources, and questions about the quality of higher education have produced a louder call for evidence of the effectiveness of programs and services as pressure from internal and external stakeholders has increased (Erwin, 1991, 1993, 1996; Hyman, Beeler, & Benedict, 1994). Leadership programs are not immune to this trend.

There is no single right or wrong way to conduct assessment. Decisions about assessment should emerge as particular questions are answered: For what purpose is the assessment being conducted? How will the information produced from assessment be used? What parameters present limitations for the assessment activity? Additionally, it is important to be familiar with the differing types of assessment techniques to make informed decisions about which methods will best match the answers to the above questions.

The vast majority of assessment techniques for leadership programs are quantitative in nature, generally in the form of an instrument. The types of instruments used to measure leadership are as varied as the definitions of leadership. The most recent edition of the second volume of *Leadership Education 1996–1997: A Source Book* (Freeman, Knott, & Schwartz, 1996) reported a compilation of 73 leadership inventories and questionnaires, all with some indication of instrument reliability, validity, and developmental foundation. Another collection of inventories, questionnaires, and surveys includes 16 tools to measure aspects of leadership including locus of control, learning, management styles, motivation, and supervision (Pfeiffer, 1994). Moreover, 56 instruments emerged from a search conducted by Snyder-Nepo (1993) to identify assessment instruments measuring leadership.

The numbers and examples of leadership instruments mentioned above seem to indicate that there is no shortage of tools to measure leadership. However, the field is devoid of available leadership development measures with an application for college students. Most instruments were designed in and for the business community with a focus on leadership that is leader-centric or positional in nature (Snyder-Nepo, 1993). Furthermore, the language used is often not appropriate for the voluntary, informal, collaborative, and/or inclusive nature of many of the non-hierarchical leadership processes in which college students participate. Finally, too often instruments to measure leadership are difficult or expensive to obtain. As a result, many people decide to create their own questionnaires or surveys to gather the information they are seeking.

Such a situation led to my development of an instrument to operationalize the Social Change Model of Leadership Development. This model of non-hierarchical leadership has become very popular around the country as a new way to think about leadership development for college students. It has been the topic of many conference sessions, the buzz on leadership development listservs, and the focus of articles in professional publications (Astin, 1996). However, no measurement existed to determine the extent to which students participated in this process of leadership. Thus, my dissertation research produced a valid and reliable instrument, named the Socially Responsible Leadership Scale, to measure the Social Change Model (Tyree, 1998).

DEVELOPING AN INSTRUMENT

To develop an instrument requires thoughtful planning and construction. In developing an instrument for research, several steps must be completed with great rigor to ensure that the data being collected are solid. However, for an instrument that is to be used for assessment purposes, time or financial resources may dictate appropriate modifications to the process. Presented here are a few important steps in the instrument development process. Several of the resources listed in the references at the end of the chapter provide greater detail about this process.

The first step in the assessment process is to identify what is to be assessed. The goals and intended outcomes of a program may serve as focal points for determining the purpose of the assessment (Erwin, 1996). Effective program goals should specify "the knowledge students will learn, the competencies necessary for success, and the expected developmental outcomes" (Erwin, 1996, p. 418). The assessment of non-hierarchical leadership may be more fruitful if it concentrates on what students are to gain, develop, or accomplish, instead of the specific programs or services offered.

The CAS Standards for Student Leadership Programs (Miller, 1997) provide a helpful guide to assessing student leadership programs. In general, the *CAS Book of Professional Standards for Higher Education* is intended to "develop and promulgate standards of professional practice to guide practitioners and their institutions, especially in their work with college students" (p. 1). In 1997, specific standards for student leadership programs were designed with leadership conceptualized as a non-hierarchical process inclusive of all students. The standards and guidelines present a framework for a comprehensive approach to the establishment of new, or the review of existing, non-hierarchical leadership programs.

The focus for the Socially Responsible Leadership Scale was the values of the leadership process identified in the Social Change Model of Leadership Development. The Seven Cs and *Change* became the eight constructs for measurement. In addition to choosing what was to be measured, other decisions had to be made: For whom was the instrument being designed and for what purpose was the instrument to be used? The Socially Responsible Leadership Scale was developed for use by all college students, as this was the target population of the Social Change Model. Furthermore, the instrument was intended to be used with individuals, informal groups, or more formal organizations, in both research and practice application, and for a multitude of purposes. Finally, the instrument needed to be "self-scoring, user friendly, easily administered and interpreted, fairly short and concise, and easily read and understood" (Tyree, 1998, p. 75).

After determining the focus for assessment, the investigator or person conducting the assessment study must generate items (questions or statements to which the participant responds) for the instrument (DeVellis, 1991; Spector, 1992). What should be asked? How should items be worded? What order should be given? Ideally, the pool of items begins large and is narrowed through data collection and analysis. However, for assessment purposes, items are often developed and used immediately, without further testing. The following guidelines are particularly important to create high quality items that are clear, concise, and unambiguous (Spector, 1992).

First, items should express a single idea. Items that represent two different ideas (sometimes called double-barreled items) are likely to be confusing (DeVellis, 1991; Spector, 1992). Someone taking the instrument will be unsure how to respond if he or she does not feel identically about both ideas. Similarly, exceptionally long items should be avoided (DeVellis, 1991). While the intent is not to lose meaning or context, unnecessary wordiness increases complexity and diminishes clarity.

The choice of words and construction of ideas must be considered when writing items (DeVellis, 1991; Spector, 1992). The reading level, vocabulary, and complexity of thought should be appropriate for the intended respondents. Such things as multiple negatives, ambiguous pronoun references, misplaced modifiers, and the use of adjective forms instead of nouns can all create confusion when reading the items (DeVellis, 1991). Additionally colloquialisms, slang, and jargon should not be used for risk of limiting the instrument to a select population or specific time span (Spector, 1992). It is best for items to contain language that is as generalizable as possible. This would include the use of language that embraces a diverse population of respondents. Care should always be given to writing items that are free of biased language. The use of non-inclusive language has proven to be a problem with many leadership instruments (Snyder-Nepo, 1993).

After items are generated, an order for the items must be established. Sudman and Bradburn (1982) suggest several major "check points" for making order decisions. First, it is best to begin with easier, non-threatening questions to get the respondents comfortable with the instrument. More difficult or threatening questions should come nearer the end. If the instrument is comprised of several topics, the items should be grouped by topics such that respondents complete all items for one topic before moving to a new one. It is helpful to introduce each topic with a heading or transitional statement. Moreover, if the format for responding to items changes, cluster the similar items together and provide directions for each type. Finally, it is usually best to put demographic questions at the end of the instrument. There is potential for respondents to feel threatened by these questions.

At the same time items are being developed, the investigator must make decisions about response choices for the items. Of the several response formats possible in an instrument, three are most popular: agreement, frequency, and evaluation (Spector, 1992). Agreement response choices ask the respondent to indicate along some continuum the degree to which they agree or disagree with a statement. Respondents indicate the number of times something happened or should happen in a frequency response format, with choice indicated numerically (once, twice) or verbally (rarely, always, some of the time). Finally, using an evaluation response format, participants respond to items along a good-bad continuum, with "terrible" and "excellent" as examples of end points.

While many other steps may be necessary depending on the complexity of the instrument or study, these general guidelines are a helpful starting point for designing an instrument. If the assessment study is to be conducted with an instrument developed by someone else, the above guidelines are a good tool for "checking" the instrument. Many instruments are distributed and used widely that have poorly written items and report no validity or reliability statistics. In her review of 56 leadership instruments, Snyder-Nepo (1993) found little available information to support their validity or reliability. Instruments with little or no indication of validity should be used with caution.

Development of the Socially Responsible Leadership Scale was a much more rigorous process than described above, as the scale was intended to be widely used in connection with the Social Change Model for research and assessment. The research included three phases of data collection and several statistical tests to determine the strength of the items. Items were removed in each testing phase to produce a solid set of final items. The results affirmed its preliminary use in assessment activities. Instruments, however, are rarely "finished." As the instrument is used, statistical analyses will continue to be performed with new data, new students, and new leadership situations. (For more detail on this research and the development of the Socially Responsible Leadership Scale, see Tyree, 1998.)

ADMINISTERING THE INSTRUMENT

After a solid set of items are compiled, the instrument is ready for use. Instruments can be administered in a number of ways. When making this decision, it is helpful to consider the resources available for the study. Salant and Dillman (1994) recommend five questions that may guide this decision:

1. How many people are available to help with the administration and what kind of experience do they have?
2. How much time can be committed to producing the results?
3. Is there someone available to help with instrumentation experience and what would be the cost?
4. What facilities are necessary and available (e.g., telephones)?
5. How much money can be spent on the administration of the instrument?

A common method of administration is to have each participant complete a pencil-and-paper instrument in person or by mail. The response rate of a face-to-face administration tends to be higher than a mailed one because respondents are a captive audience and less likely to discard the instrument. It is also an advantage to be able to give instructions in person, particularly if they are complicated (Sudman & Bradburn, 1982). Furthermore, there is little concern that a respondent will consult another person (assuming those directions are given) when providing answers. Giving an instrument in person, however, can be difficult because it is fairly time intensive for the investigator, and a sample of the population of interest may not be readily available when and where they are needed. Also, obtaining a random sample, if important to the study, is challenging. Finally, for issues of a more personal or threatening topic, the anonymity provided by mailed instruments is preferable (Sudman & Bradburn, 1982).

Telephone surveys are also used frequently in assessment. According to Suskie, response rates are almost always higher with telephone surveys than with administering an instrument in person or by mail (as cited in Upcraft & Schuh,

1996). It is possible to reach a broader participant group while creating the personal contact that encourages people to participate. Another advantage of telephone administration is that the data can be collected more cheaply (unless several long distance calls are necessary) and quickly (Sudman & Bradburn, 1982; Upcraft & Schuh, 1996). The ability of the investigator to respond to the unanticipated makes using the telephone more desirable than the mail, but consistency in delivery and recording responses may create concerns. Telephone calling also excludes potential participants who do not have phones, have unlisted numbers, or do not have correct number listed with the providing source (e.g., an institutional phone directory). This can be particularly problematic when assessing college students who tend to move often.

As colleges and universities have greater technological capacities, Web-based questionnaires are becoming increasingly popular (Tyree, 1997). There are several advantages to this use of technology, including students' interest in the Web, the ability to save time and money in data collection, and the ability to create an automated data entry process. However, this type of administration is not without concerns. Consideration must be given to the members of the desired population who do not have access to the Web. Additionally, there is the possibility of "sampling and response bias, technical difficulties, and respondent anonymity" (Tyree, 1997, p. 10).

Each of these procedures for instrument administration has its strengths and weaknesses. The nature of the assessment and information to be gathered will influence which procedure is best.

In studies of non-hierarchical leadership programs, quantitative methods of inquiry are preferable when information is desired from larger numbers of students. Moreover, administering an instrument can be useful if fiscal and human resources are limited. However, it can be time consuming to create a good instrument if one is not already available. Additionally, there are times when an instrument does not answer the question that is being asked. Qualitative methods of inquiry may be the preferred approach to gain the desired information in these cases.

COLLECTING DATA QUALITATIVELY

In contrast with quantitative methods, qualitative studies often involve smaller numbers of participants, provide more detailed information, and are not conducted with an intent of being generalizable to other populations or settings. They may be a more effective approach when assessing campus-based leadership programs and activities. The purpose of the information gathered through qualitative methods is to make meaning of participants' lives, experiences, or interpretations of situations (Creswell, 1994; Erwin, 1996; Merriam, 1988).

While quantitative methods of inquiry rely on instruments for data collection and analysis, qualitative research is dependent upon the investigator him- or herself to be the primary data collection instrument (Erwin, 1996; Merriam,

1988). This often provides some of the greatest excitement and challenges of the process. When engaging in a qualitative assessment, the person(s) conducting the analysis must be prepared to commit a significant amount of time and energy to engage in a dynamic and time consuming process.

Qualitative inquiry produces large units of data; however, there is no statistical analysis to provide understanding of the data. It is a greater challenge in qualitative inquiry to "make sense of massive amounts of data, reduce the volume of information, identify significant patterns, and construct a framework for communicating the essence of what the data reveal" (Patton, 1990, pp. 371–372). The investigator engages in an inductive analysis of the data to make meaning of the information (Merriam, 1988; Patton, 1990; Upcraft & Schuh, 1996). Themes, patterns, and categories should emerge to illuminate the phenomenon and paint a picture or tell a story. The interpretation of these themes results in "attaching significance to what was found, offering explanations, drawing conclusions, extrapolating lessons, making inferences, building linkages, attaching meanings, imposing order, and dealing with rival explanations, disconfirming cases, and data irregularities as part of testing the viability of an interpretation" (Patton, 1990, p. 423). It is important to remember that the interpretation does not yield the same type of results as a quantitative analysis. The object of the assessment should be better understood, but the data will not usually determine causation, predict, or allow for generalizations.

Qualitative methods of inquiry are better used in some evaluative settings than others. For example, they are often more useful than quantitative methods in making meaning of something that has happened or understanding the process by which it happened (Merriam, 1988; Patton, 1990). Additionally, qualitative methods are often advantageous when the investigator is interested in the individualized impact of a program or intervention for which a greater depth of analysis is preferable. Sometimes both qualitative and quantitative approaches are beneficial or necessary to understand fully the phenomenon of interest.

Although some people resist using qualitative forms of analysis because these methods are thought to be more complicated and time intensive than distributing a survey and tabulating the results, the depth and richness of the information may be worth the effort. Additionally, qualitative studies do not have to be complicated if the assessment process is well-planned and executed. The use of qualitative methods for evaluative purposes was expressed by Patton (1990) as simply a process in which a person must "pay attention, listen and watch, be open, think about what you hear and see, document systematically (memory is selective and unreliable), and apply what you learn" (p. 138). Three kinds of techniques for data collection which might be particularly useful in assessing non-hierarchical leadership include interviews and focus groups, direct observation, and document analysis.

Interviews are one-to-one interactions which provide participants the ability to respond in their own words and express personal perspectives on the topic of interest (Patton, 1990). In qualitative interviewing, questions are usually open-ended and probing to obtain information that cannot be observed directly. "The data from interviews consist of direct quotations from people about their experiences, opinions, feelings, and knowledge" (Patton, 1990, p. 10). Questions should be singular in idea, straightforward, neutral, clear, and free of jargon. Technical terms should be defined at the beginning of the interview. Leading questions should be avoided to prevent directing a participant toward a particular response (Borg & Gall, 1989).

Interviews need to be well-planned so the experience is similar for each of the respondents. An interview guide with a list of questions to be addressed in the interview may be beneficial (Patton, 1990). This will help structure the limited amount of time in the interview and identify the topics or subject areas that the investigator wants to illuminate. Additionally, a training session may be valuable to increase consistency if several people will assist with interviewing.

Focus groups are interviews with small groups of people, typically six to eight at one time, who participate collectively in an interview for one-half to two hours (Patton, 1990). This is possibly the most commonly used method of qualitative analysis in student affairs assessment. The data resulting from focus groups differ from that of a collection of individual interviews in that participants will react to and build upon the responses of others (Stewart & Shamdasani, 1990).

Additionally, the investigator in a focus group may serve more in the role of moderator than interviewer. The moderator will guide participants through the discussion, playing a somewhat less active role than in the interview as participants feed off each other (Kaase & Harshbarger, 1993). A moderator should summarize group consensus occasionally without oversimplifying or negating the value of differences of opinion. A record of the entire interview is necessary for later interpretation. Three options exist for recording the interview: a note taker, an audio recording, and a video recording. Data may be collected using a single mechanism or some combination.

A second technique for qualitative inquiry is direct observation. Inquiry by observation can provide insight to help understand the complexities of a situation that interviews or surveys may not elucidate (Patton, 1990). Observations can be as unintrusive as simply watching people's behaviors, or the investigator may actually participate in the activity of interest (known as participant observation). "The data from observations consist of detailed descriptions of people's activities, behaviors, actions, and the full range of interpersonal interactions and organizational processes that are part of observable human experience" (Patton, 1990, p. 10). As the observer records the details of the setting, the experiences of the participants, and the meanings of what is observed, he or she must be factual and thorough, without becoming overwhelmed with trivial detail. Observations can be useful in assessment, particularly when evaluating a program with which the investigator is unfamiliar. Sometimes the only way to gain a deeper understanding of a situation or event is to participate and observe. Additionally, the observer may discover things that participants are too close to see themselves or are unwilling to discuss in an interview (Patton, 1990). It is important for the observer to allow time for reflection and introspection to process the experience. The reactions, impressions, and feelings of the investigator become important to provide greater depth to the evaluation.

A more indirect or passive form of qualitative inquiry, document analysis is used to collect rich information not available through other methods of data collection. "The data from document analysis in qualitative inquiry yields excerpts, quotations, or entire passages from organizational, clinical, or program records; memoranda and correspondence; official publications and reports; personal diaries; and open-ended written responses to questionnaires and surveys" (Patton, 1990, p. 10). Documents may take the form of personal or official records. Document analysis may be used to generate questions to be explored through direct observation or interviews. However, document analysis is often not as valuable a form of data collection by itself as it is in combination with other methods. While it can provide information that may never be verbalized, it is unidirectional and may leave the investigator with an unclear, incomplete or inaccurate picture of the phenomenon (Merriam, 1988; Patton, 1990; Upcraft & Schuh, 1996).

Using multiple forms of data collection often helps overcome the limitations of a single technique and provides a more comprehensive picture of the issue of interest (Evans, 1985; Patton, 1990). It also helps to crosscheck the information that is collected. A multifaceted procedure, however, can be costly and time consuming. While some questions can be answered with a simpler approach, assessments that lead to policy changes, budgetary decisions, or other significant decisions, may be well worth the investment.

USING THE ASSESSMENT RESULTS

The possibilities for use of the assessment results are as varied as the purposes. Using the results, however, may be one of the most challenging aspects of the entire process (Erwin, 1996). The purpose for collecting and the plan for utilizing the information should have been determined in advance. At the point of making decisions or implementing change based on the results, it is particularly beneficial to have had all stakeholders involved from the outset. Furthermore, modeling a non-hierarchical leadership process in the dissemination of the information may lead to more positive and productive results.

Assessment is often thought to be a top-down, hierarchical process. Accountability comes from senior administrators, legislators, accrediting bodies, boards of trustees, and others who set expectations for academic units, services, and programs of the college or university. Department chairs mobilize faculty and/ or staff members to assemble the information requested from above. The people collecting the data may feel powerless and unable to effect real change in a process that is dictated from the top. This example of an assessment process closely reflects more traditional theories of leadership development, which contradict many of the non-hierarchical principles presented in this book.

However, using Upcraft and Schuh's (1996) rules for making good use of results as a framework, non-hierarchical leadership principles can be integrated easily into the assessment process. First, it is important that the assessment study is needed and desired—something to which others will pay attention. Assessments that have no impact are often those that produce results for which stakeholders were not prepared. However, utilizing a collaborative approach to assessment will increase the likelihood that all stakeholders feel a sense of ownership in the process and results.

Second, it is critical to determine the degree to which the study is confidential. While this question should be addressed in advance, it becomes particularly important at the time of utilizing results. Questions of confidentiality raise the issues of who knows the study is being conducted and who has access to the results. There are situations in which limited access to results is very important. However, information is seen too often as power, and confidentiality simply becomes a control mechanism. By adopting a non-hierarchical approach, information will be distributed broadly and credited appropriately whenever possible. Sharing assessment information can empower those who work hard to implement a program or deliver a service and allow them to feel ownership in the process.

A third important rule for making the most of results includes determining who should be involved in the study. As ideas for the study begin to take shape, those involved in the investigation and decision making should be committed to the project. Trust and confidence between the investigator and those affected should be enhanced. Moreover, adopting an approach that is inclusive of as many people as possible, gathered around a common purpose, models a principle highly valued in non-hierarchical leadership.

The fourth rule for utilizing results is to conduct a good study. While seemingly obvious, the quality of the study is likely to have a significant impact on the usefulness of the information produced. There are still many critics of leadership programs and the idea of leadership as a developmental process. Knowing who these people are, and possibly getting them involved, will ultimately strengthen the leadership program on the campus. Utilizing a non-hierarchical leadership approach may serve to minimize potential conflict. Listening sincerely to others and valuing ideas different from one's own can allow for controversy with civility, one of the principles of the Social Change Model of Leadership (Higher Education Research Institute [HERI], 1996), and better outcomes in the long run.

Writing a good report is another important rule for using results of an assessment study. It does not matter how good the assessment is if the report is not readable, understandable, approachable, and interesting. Knowing one's audience is critical to writing a report that will be embraced by the "right" people. After completing the report, the investigator should be prepared to implement a dissemination plan. It is important that all parties invested in the assessment (e.g., the investigator and key decision makers) are in agreement with the dissemination plan. With a non-hierarchical leadership program, interested parties might include alumni/ae, parents, or colleagues at other institutions. Having more people invested in the program will set up a stronger network of support for new ideas and changes that result from the data.

The final rule for effective utilization of results is to develop a plan for using the report. On occasion, all of the above rules are followed and a terrific assessment is completed. Then, no one assumes responsibility for ensuring that the results are used. The investigator, principal decision makers, and those impacted by the results should determine collaboratively when and how the information will be incorporated into the decision-making process (Upcraft & Schuh, 1996). For a leadership program, the report might be used for program improvement, budgetary decisions, long-range planning, or resource allocation.

Following these rules and embracing a non-hierarchical leadership process will improve the likelihood for success in the utilization of assessment results. If the assessment is in response to calls for greater accountability, a thorough assessment, inclusive of meaningful reporting and use of results, is more likely to lead to a positive outcome. Additionally, in keeping with the essence of non-hierarchical leadership development, effective assessment will produce a broader range of leadership opportunities that are inclusive of a greater diversity of students.

CONCLUSION

This chapter is intended to provide an introduction to the importance of and options for assessing non-hierarchical leadership. Once the investigator decides to conduct an assessment and identifies a technique for data collection, other resources will become necessary to provide a step-by-step outline of the assessment process. While many references are available to assist with assessment processes, *Assessing Student Learning and Development* (Erwin, 1991) and *Assessment in Student Affairs* (Upcraft & Schuh, 1996) are particularly helpful. They are more general guides to conducting assessment, but are quite applicable to non-hierarchical leadership development and programs. Adopting principles of non-hierarchical leadership in the assessment process will lead to more effective results and positive change.

REFERENCES

Astin, H. S. (1996, July–August). Leadership for social change. *About Campus, 1*, 4–10.
Borg, W. R., & Gall, M. D. (1989). *Educational research: An introduction* (5th ed.). White Plains, NY: McKay.

Creswell, J. W. (1994). *Research design: Qualitative and quantitative approaches.* Thousand Oaks, CA: Sage.

DeVellis, R. F. (1991). *Scale development: Theory and applications.* Newbury Park, CA: Sage.

Erwin, T. D. (1991). *Assessing student learning and development: A guide to the principles, goals, and methods of determining college outcomes.* San Francisco: Jossey-Bass.

Erwin, T. D. (1993). Outcomes assessment. In M. J. Barr et al. (Eds.), *The handbook of student affairs* (pp. 230–241). San Francisco: Jossey-Bass.

Erwin, T. D. (1996). Assessment, evaluation, and research. In S. R. Komives & D. B. Woodard, Jr., et al. (Eds.), *Student services: A handbook for the profession* (3rd ed., pp. 415–432). San Francisco: Jossey-Bass.

Evans, N. J. (1985). Needs assessment methodology: A comparison of results. *Journal of College Student Personnel, 26,* 107–114.

Freeman, F. H., Knott, K. B., & Schwartz, M. K. (Eds.). (1996). *Leadership education 1996–1997: A source book. Vol. 2: Leadership resources* (6th ed.). Greensboro, NC: Center for Creative Leadership.

Higher Education Research Institute. (1996). *A Social Change Model of Leadership Development* (3rd ed.). Los Angeles: Author.

Hyman, R. E., Beeler, K. J., & Benedict, L. G. (1994). Outcomes assessment and student affairs: New roles and expectations. *NASPA Journal, 32,* 20–30.

Kaase, K. J., & Harshbarger, D. B. (1993). Applying focus groups in student affairs assessment. *NASPA Journal, 30,* 284–289.

Merriam, S. B. (1988). *Case study research in education: A qualitative approach.* San Francisco: Jossey-Bass.

Miller, T. K. (Ed.). (1997). *CAS: The book of professional standards for higher education* (2nd ed.). Washington, DC: Council for the Advancement of Standards in Higher Education.

Patrick, J., & Niles, S. G. (1988). Establishing accountability and evaluation procedures in student affairs offices. *NASPA Journal, 25,* 291–296.

Patton, M. Q. (1990). *Qualitative evaluation and research methods* (2nd ed.). Newbury Park, CA: Sage.

Pfeiffer, J. W. (Ed.). (1994). *Library of inventories, questionnaires, and surveys: Leadership* (Vol. 19). Amsterdam: Pfeiffer.

Salant, P., & Dillman, D. A. (1994). *How to conduct your own survey.* New York: John Wiley & Sons.

Snyder-Nepo, N. (1993). *Leadership assessments: A critique of common instruments.* College Park, MD: National Clearinghouse for Leadership Programs.

Spector, P. E. (1992). *Summated rating scale construction: An introduction.* Newbury Park, CA: Sage.

Stewart, D. W., & Shamdasani, P. N. (1990). *Focus groups: Theory and practice.* Newbury Park, CA: Sage.

Sudman, S., & Bradburn, N. M. (1982). *Asking questions: A practical guide to questionnaire design.* San Francisco: Jossey-Bass.

Tyree, T. (1997, October). Assessing with the net: Using technology to know more about students. *AAHE Bulletin, 50*(2), 10–12.

Tyree, T. M. (1998). *Designing an instrument to measure socially responsible leadership using the Social Change Model of Leadership Development*. Unpublished doctoral dissertation, University of Maryland, College Park.

Upcraft, M. L., & Schuh, J. H. (1996). *Assessment in student affairs: A guide for practitioners*. San Francisco: Jossey-Bass.

Index

About the Contributors

DANIEL C. ADAMS is Assistant Director for Leadership Education for the Office of Student Activities and Leadership at the University of Michigan.

JACQUELYN ALEXANDER is Dean of the School of Education and Clinical Studies and Director of the Center for Leadership Studies at Our Lady of the Lake University in San Antonio, Texas. She has held multiple offices in Texas and national professional associations, and is currently the Vice President for the Council for Exceptional Children.

KATHLEEN ALLEN is a Senior Fellow at the University of Maryland's Academy of Leadership. She has worked in higher education for over 28 years at a variety of colleges and universities. She has written and presented widely on leadership and both human and organizational development. She is co-author (with Cynthia Cherrey) of *Systemic Leadership: Enriching the Meaning of Our Work.*

HEATHER ANDERSON is a Wellness Educator and Program Advisor in the Office of Student Life at Paradise Valley Community College in Phoenix, Arizona.

PATRICIA M. AQUI is a mediator, facilitator, and human relations educator at Washington State University. Through her work, she has opportunities to build communities of difference with students, faculty and staff members throughout the institution. She believes that community is built through the dynamic interplay of human differences *and* similarities.

ALEXANDER W. ASTIN is Allan M. Cartter Professor of Education and Director of the Higher Education Research Institute at UCLA. He is the author of 18 books, including *Maximizing Leadership Effectiveness* (with Rita Scherrei) and co-author (with Helen S. Astin) of the guidebook *A Social Change Model of Leadership Development*.

HELEN S. ASTIN is Professor of Higher Education and Associate Director of the Higher Education Research Institute at UCLA. She has been honored with the Award for Outstanding Contribution to Research and Literature by the National Association of Student Personnel Administrators and was named Distinguished Leader for Women in Psychology by the American Psychological Association's Committee on Women in Psychology. Dr. Astin's major books include *Women of Influence, Women of Vision*; *Human Resources and Higher Education*; *The Women Doctorate in America*; *Women: A Bibliography on Their Education and Careers*; and *Sex Roles: An Annotated Research Bibliography*.

NETTA AVINERI was born in Israel and moved to America at the age of two. Currently a third-year linguistic anthropology major and a French minor at UCLA, she hopes to become a professor and is involved in many on-campus organizations at UCLA.

DIANE BISCHETTI coordinates community service programs at Loyola Marymount University. Diane has been active in promoting social justice for women. Prior to LMU, she oversaw the sexual violence prevention program at UCLA using a peer education model. Her volunteer work has included working with incarcerated youth and women.

MARGUERITE BONOUS-HAMMARTH is a Research Associate in Higher Education and Organizational Change at the UCLA Graduate School of Education & Information Studies. Her teaching and research interests examine factors that foster successful student outcomes and academic communities, including issues related to person-organization fit, life span influences on college students, and sustaining organizational change efforts.

RAY BORYCZKA is Assistant Director of the Center for Leadership Studies at Our Lady of the Lake University. During his 30-year career he has served in various faculty and administrative positions in public and private universities. His numerous publications and scholarly contributions have focused on American social history.

CHRISTOPHER S. CHAMBERS is Assistant Dean/Special Assistant to the Dean of Residential Life at Dartmouth College and a doctoral student in Social Justice Education at UMass-Amherst. His interests include leadership theory, multiculturalism, and organizational change. He has been involved with leadership programs at the University of Maryland and Dartmouth and served as a faculty member for LeaderShape Inc.

CYNTHIA CHERREY is Assistant Vice President for Student Affairs and Clinical Associate Professor at the University of Southern California. She has published in various professional journals and consults with profit and non-profit organizations. She serves on the Board of Directors for the International Leadership Association and is a Fulbright Scholar.

CHRISTINE M. CRESS is Assistant Professor in the Postsecondary, Adult, and Continuing Education program in the Graduate School of Education at Portland State University. She has over a decade of experience with student affairs work in community colleges and universities. She is also an Affiliated Scholar of the Higher Education Research Institute (UCLA).

PAUL DALE is Dean of Students at Paradise Valley Community College.

FRED DANSEREAU is Associate Professor of Organization and Human Resources in the School of Management at the State University of New York at Buffalo. Dr. Dansereau has extensive experience in the areas of leadership and managing at the individual, group, and collective levels of analysis. He has published 4 books and over 60 articles, is a consultant to various organizations, and serves as Associate Editor of the journal *Group and Organization Management*.

SHANNON K. FARIS is a consultant at Public Works, Inc., a private non-profit public policy and education consulting firm in Pasadena, CA. While a doctoral student at UCLA, she co-founded the Bruin Leaders Project. In addition to non-hierarchical leadership development and theory, her research interests include student development in college students, entrepreneurism in education, and educational policy and reform at the K–12 level.

ROGER FISHER is the Associate Director of the Multi-Ethnic Student Affairs unit at the University of Michigan. His undergraduate and graduate experiences at the University of Michigan took place during the very volatile and influential time of the institution's adoption of its mandate regarding ethnic minorities and women. He translated those student experiences into a professional commitment and dedication to multicultural and social justice education.

CHRISTOPHER R. FOLEY is currently a Graduate Assistant and doctoral student in the Center for the Study of Higher Education at the University of Virginia. Previously he was the Associate Dean of Students at King's College in Wilkes-Barre, Pennsylvania and an Area Director at Dartmouth College in Hanover, New Hampshire.

JUDI BIGGS GARBUIO is Assistant Dean of Students/Director of Leadership, Service, and Scholars at the University of Southern California. Judi has worked with a variety of leadership programs during her fifteen years within Student Affairs. Most recently she created the Emerging Leader Program and co-facilitated the development of Your Portfolio, which are highlighted in her chapter.

MARK T. GREEN is a former Major in the U.S. Army and is the Chair of the Doctoral Program in Leadership Studies at Our Lady of the Lake University.

SARAH J. HANSEN is a political science student at UCLA. Graduating in June 2000, she is pursuing a career in print journalism and has worked for the *Los Angeles Times*, the *Daily Bruin*, and *FEM* magazine. Sarah's active involvement in campus life includes marching band and the Bruin Leaders Project.

NANCY S. HUBER is Associate Professor, Department of Agricultural Education at the University of Arizona. As a leadership educator she may be found in the classroom, in board rooms, at conferences, and in community meeting places. She teaches from the heart, modeling her beliefs concerning the integration of learning and leading.

RACHEL ISGAR is an Assistant to the Vice President for Student Affairs at the University of Southern California. Rachel has worked in a variety of offices at USC in addition to Student Affairs, including athletics, education, and public administration. Most recently she co-authored an article on leadership with Cynthia Cherrey called "Leadership Education in the Context of the New Millennium."

TAMMERA J. KLUMPYAN is the Director of Student Involvement and Campus Activities in the Department of Leadership, Service and Involvement at St. Norbert College in Green Bay, Wisconsin.

EMILY A. LANGDON is Associate Dean for Leadership Development and Education at St. Norbert College. She teaches two courses in the interdisciplinary Leadership Studies minor—the introduction course and the senior capstone seminar—and oversees the co-curricular department of Leadership, Service and Involvement.

MARY LISCINSKY is Special Assistant to the Dean of the College at Dartmouth College. She has a special interest in contextual leadership, especially in determining what mode of leadership will work at specific universities.

BRYAN J. LUBIC is a Graduate Teaching Associate in the School of Communication at San Diego State University. He has served as the Graduate Assistant for Leadership Programs in the Student Resource Center. His current research projects are focusing on classroom and instructional interaction.

JOE MANKO is a third-year undergraduate studying history, political science, and education at UCLA. He has explored the concept of non-hierarchical leadership through his involvement in the Bruin Leaders Project.

SUNSHINE B. MARTIN is the Coordinator of Student Activities and Campus-Wide Events at the University of Nevada, Las Vegas.

NANCY B. MATHIAS is Associate Director of Leadership and Service at St. Norbert College. She is an experiential educator who utilizes both the ropes course and community service as teaching tools. She was also a member of the SNC Eisenhower grant team that developed the "Application Guidebook" for the Social Change Model.

KATHLEEN N. McMAHON is Assistant Dean of Students, and co-staff and co-founder of the Bruin Leaders Project at UCLA. Her doctoral research focused on leadership development, in which she developed a prototypical model for a leadership program for female college students. Her background in social work continues to be the foundation of her interest in the psychological development of college students, and women students in particular. At UCLA her roles include education and awareness training concerning issues of sexual harassment, sexual assault, and academic integrity, and student grievances and advocacy.

WAYNE R. MILLETTE is Assistant Professor in Education and Director of the Master of Arts in Teaching program at Olivet College in Michigan. He most recently served as Assistant Director for Leadership Education at the University of Michigan.

As Assistant Dean of Students at UCLA, CHARLES L. OUTCALT co-founded, with Shannon Faris and Kathleen McMahon, the Bruin Leaders Project, a non-hierarchical student leadership program based on the Social Change Model of Leadership Development. As a Ph.D. candidate in Higher Education, he is a Spencer Foundation Predoctoral Research Fellow specializing in the role of community colleges in promoting educational equity. His student affairs publications and presentations have concerned leadership development and diversity within higher education. His research publications and presentations have focused on educational access, sociological theory, Historically Black Colleges and Universities, and educational entrepreneurship.

DENNIS C. ROBERTS is Assistant Vice President for Student Affairs at Miami University in Oxford, Ohio. He co-edited *Student Leadership Programs in Higher Education* in 1981. He is a past president of the American College

Personnel Association and received one of its 75th Anniversary Diamond Awards in 1999.

DAVID C. ROBERTSON is Associate Director of the Student Resource Center at San Diego State University. He has taught the leadership course and directed leadership programs for over ten years. His current projects include helping to establish a Center for Community-Based Service Learning and continuing to develop the leadership class.

JAMES RUBIN serves as personal and career counselor and faculty instructor of personal development courses at Paradise Valley Community College.

RONNI SANLO is Director of the UCLA LGBT Campus Resource Center and Chair of the National Consortium of LGBT Campus Resource Center Directors. She is the author of *Unheard Voices: The Effects of Silence on Lesbian and Gay Educators* and the editor of *Working with Lesbian, Gay, Bisexual, and Transgender College Students*, both published by Greenwood Press.

CINDY SHOENHAIR is an exercise physiologist and faculty instructor of wellness, health, exercise science, and physical education courses at Paradise Valley Community College.

JENNIFER SU is a senior at UCLA, majoring in international economics with a concentration in East Asian studies. She has been part of the Bruin Leaders Project facilitation team for two years.

TRACY M. TYREE is Director of the First Year Experience and Academic Advising Center at Mercer University in Macon, Georgia. Her interest in non-hierarchical leadership stems from her doctoral experience at the University of Maryland. Tracy developed an instrument to operationalize the Social Change Model of Leadership Development for her dissertation research.

LORI E. VARLOTTA is Assistant Vice President for Student Affairs at the University of San Francisco. As both a theorist and practitioner, Dr. Varlotta has creatively conceptualized and operationalized key components of American higher education. Recently, her work has contributed nuances to the ways educators think about, talk about, and do "community," "service," and "leadership."

SHELLE WITTEN is a faculty reference and instruction librarian at Paradise Valley Community College.

FRANCIS J. YAMMARINO is Professor of Management and Fellow and Associate Director of the Center for Leadership Studies at the State University of

New York at Binghamton. His research and consulting interests include superior–subordinate relationships, leadership, self-other agreement processes, and multiple levels of analysis issues.

MARIANA ZAVALA-CORZO is Director of Programs at the International Student Center, UCLA, with which she has been involved for eight years. She has lived and studied in Mexico, Brazil, Italy, and the United States and is involved in diversity, leadership, and lesbian/gay/bisexual/transgender organizations through UCLA, NAFSA, and NASPA.